BEHAVIOUR PROBLEMS IN SCHOOLS

Behaviour Problems in Schools

An Evaluation of Support Centres

**Peter Mortimore, Jean Davies,
Andreas Varlaam and Anne West
with Patricia Devine and Julia Mazza**

CROOM HELM
London & Canberra

© 1983 Peter Mortimore, Jean Davies, Anne West, Andreas
Varlaam, Patricia Devine and Julia Mazza
Croom Helm Ltd, Provident House, Burrell Row,
Beckenham, Kent BR3 1AT
Croom Helm Australia Pty Ltd, 28 Kembla Street,
Fyshwick, ACT 2609, Australia

British Library Cataloguing in Publication Data

Behaviour problems in schools: an evaluation of
    support centres.
    1. Problem children – Education – England
    I. Mortimore, Peter
    371.94   LB3013

ISBN 0-7099-1770-8

Printed and bound in Great Britain by
Biddles Ltd, Guildford and King's Lynn

CONTENTS

FIGURES

Figures

TABLES

Tables

FOREWORD

Disruptive behaviour in schools is not a new problem. The difficulties which arise from anti-social behaviour by pupils are widely known. What may be less appreciated is the extent to which teachers are trying to deal with the various forms of disruptive behaviour. All classroom misbehaviour poses problems for at least two people; one is the pupil and the other is the teacher. It is the breakdown in this key relationship, albeit temporarily, which is crucial to an understanding of the issue. Invariably, however, the problem does not stop there since the learning processes of the other pupils may also be disturbed. Fortunately, on most occasions an experienced teacher can deal with misbehaviour and ensure that a normal atmosphere is restored. There are other instances, however, when the causes of the breakdown in relationships are so serious that it is necessary, in everyone's interests, to remove the pupil from the classroom. This means that additional forms of support must be made available to provide for the pupil outside the classroom while a long-term solution is being found.

The Inner London Education Authority has long recognised this need for additional support and has provided resources to help schools. For many years, the Authority supported such additional educational provision as school sanctuaries, educational guidance centres, intermediate treatment schemes, voluntary agency centres and home tuition. With the ending of selection in Inner London, in 1978, it was necessary to ensure that all secondary schools were organised to cope with any serious behaviour problems. In the ensuing discussions, heads and teachers asked the Authority to provide additional support and, as a consequence, a major school support programme was launched with the aim of co-ordinating and, where necessary, expanding the various forms of support available to teachers and schools in dealing with disruptive behaviour. As part of this initiative, the Research and Statistics Branch of the Authority was asked to monitor the programme's implementation and development.

This book has developed out of that work. After careful analysis of what is meant by disruptive behaviour, the authors describe the different kinds of alternative provision that are available. Drawing on a number of different studies, they document what is known of the effectiveness of this provision generally. They then use the findings of the London research to evaluate this provision.

The results are interesting. The problems teachers have to face are detailed, as is the hard work and dedication of those who are working in this field. Not surprisingly the research reveals a range of innovative approaches which teachers are using to deal with disruptive behaviour.

In providing support centres, the Authority was determined to avoid establishing a separate education system isolated from schools. The authors describe the reasons behind this policy and the precautions that need to be taken to avoid such a development and give their conclusion concerning the form of alternative provision which is likely to be needed for the foreseeable future.

Whether that provision should be within the immediate surroundings of the school or elsewhere will depend very much on local circumstances, but wherever the provision is sited it is clear from experience in Inner London that careful thought must be given to maintaining the links with the main school.

Wider knowledge of this research carried out in Inner London should be useful to all those concerned with disruptive behaviour in schools.

W.H. Stubbs
Education Officer
Inner London Education Authority

PREFACE

Disruptive behaviour in school is a matter of concern to pupils, parents and teachers. If such behaviour is not contained it is bound to interfere with the learning of all children in the classroom. It is not at all clear, however, what the best way might be of dealing effectively with disruption. Over the last few years both traditional and innovative approaches have been tried. In particular, attention has been focused on 'support centres' which have developed outside both ordinary and special schools.

To date there has been little research evidence available to enable these support centres to be evaluated, or for the central issues in the discussion to be clarified. The studies which do exist have been fairly small-scale and of a predominantly descriptive nature.

Our own study has been undertaken, therefore, in the hope of providing such information as is necessary for a better understanding of the issues involved. In Chapter 1 we discuss the nature of disruptive behaviour and how it can be identified and measured; this chapter also includes a description of the various methods used for dealing with such behaviour.

Chapter 2 provides a background to the research by considering the influences on the development of support centre policy, and by assessing the extent to which they are used by LEAs. It also includes a summary of information provided by previous studies.

The aims and methods of our own research study are discussed in detail in Chapter 3. Here we describe how we came to collect our data using a mixture of quantitative and qualitative methods, in our efforts to examine and explore the complexities of life at the centres.

Chapters 4 to 7 present the main findings of our study. Chapter 4 describes the characteristics of the pupils who attend the centres, their reasons for referral and their academic performance. Chapter 5 focuses on the staff in centres including assessments of relationships between staff and pupils, and the overall atmosphere existing within centres. Chapter 6 describes what actually goes on in centres. Some of the questions considered here are: how are centres managed? how are pupils referred? and what are the teaching styles and curriculum adopted? Having established who the centre clients are, who teaches them and what actually happens to pupils when they attend, we consider, in Chapter 7, the views held by teachers in ILEA schools as to the effectiveness of support centres. Questions addressed here include: what have been the benefits and disadvantages of the centres to the pupils who attend? and how have the centres affected the pupils remaining in school or the way in which schools are managed?

Chapter 8 concludes the book with an evaluation of the centres from the point of view of pupils, teachers and schools. Here we discuss the merits and potential dangers of the support centre provision. We also highlight some of the innovative techniques found in centres which may also be of relevance within the mainstream system.

ACKNOWLEDGEMENTS

The research we present here would not have been possible without the help we have received at all stages from the staff and pupils of the centres involved. In the early stages, teachers from three centres played an active role in developing the instruments we used in the main part of the study. We are indebted to the staff and pupils of all centres for their co-operation and enthusiasm during the various parts of the research. The ideas and suggestions of teachers working in this field have done much to shape the study. We hope that they will feel that all the time and effort they have given to the research has been worthwhile.

Several research workers have been involved with the study since 1979. Peter Mortimore directed the study from the outset; Andreas Varlaam supervised it on a day-to-day basis; Jean Davies was in charge of the research team and took overall control of the design of the instruments used. Patricia Devine and Julia Mazza worked in the research team until 1981 and were involved in designing the study and in carrying out the research. Anne West has been involved since 1981 and has been primarily concerned with studying past literature and analysing the data.

We would like to thank the many people who have assisted us since 1979; Fahri Zihni for carrying out statistical analyses; Pat Bunce for organising the research team; Pat Wood and Barbara Andrews for typing several drafts of the manuscript; Lynda Lawrence and Pam Povey for help with proof reading; Owen John for advice on computing; John Wilkes for graphic material; Jo Mortimore for her advice and contributions to the various chapters; Silvana Gambini for help with the index and Joyce Clarke, Miriam Seidel and the ILEA Inspectorate for their useful advice.

Disclaimers

Chapter 1

DISRUPTIVE BEHAVIOUR IN SCHOOLS

What is disruptive behaviour? How is it identified and measured? How widespread is such behaviour at present? Have standards of behaviour fallen or risen over the last few years? What factors are associated with disruptive behaviour? How is it dealt with?

These and other similar questions are often asked by parents, anxious to choose a school in which their child will make progress and be happy; teachers, who may feel that they are having to cope with particularly difficult pupils; administrators and inspectors, who have to provide help and support for both pupils and teachers; and many others, interested in developments in our schools.

Unfortunately, although the questions are simple, the answers are not. In this chapter we present our attempts to provide satisfactory answers and, where we are unable to do so, to explain the nature of the difficulties.

What constitutes disruptive behaviour?
Some definitions of what is disruptive focus on the behaviour whilst others focus on the child. For example, in a DES study disruptive behaviour is defined as that which 'interferes with the learning and opportunities of other pupils and imposes undue stress on teachers'. In contrast, Parry (1976) defines a disruptive child as one 'who knowingly or unknowingly effectively and frequently disrupts his own education and the education of others'.

We favour the first approach and have chosen to define disruptive behaviour as any act which interferes with the learning, development or happiness of a pupil or his or her peers, or with the teacher's attempts to foster those processes or feelings. We prefer this approach as, unlike the

1

one that focuses on the pupil, it does not appear to make the pupil solely responsible for the disruptive behaviour. It allows for the fact that misbehaviour is, to a greater or lesser extent, context-bound. By this we mean that a pupil's behaviour within a classroom may be influenced by his or her peers as well as by the actions of the teacher. It is unfair, therefore, to judge the behaviour of a pupil without taking into account the context in which that behaviour takes place. Any observer who has seen a pupil change from a classroom fiend in one lesson, determined to irritate the teacher at all costs, to a compliant student in another lesson, will recognise this.

Of course, we would not wish to deny that some pupils are more likely than others to misbehave in any given situation. Quite obviously some pupils deliberately misbehave in a fashion designed to disrupt their own, or their companions' learning and their teachers' teaching. Again, other children - fortunately only a few - suffer from serious psychiatric disturbance, organic disorders, or have developmental difficulties which cause them to behave in a quite bizarre manner.(1) However, what we would like to stress by adopting a definition which focuses on the behaviour rather than the child is that many types of misbehaviour fall well within the bounds of normal behaviour. Calling out continuously, not having the correct equipment, shouting insults, acting aggressively towards other pupils, even fighting in class, are actions which can be very irritating for those pupils who are trying to concentrate on work and for teachers anxious to get on with the lesson, but they are not, by any means, an indication that the child is 'by nature' disruptive or that he or she necessarily suffers from any identifiable personality or psychiatric disorder.

---

(1) Definitions of disruptive pupils or behaviour usually exclude children who are designated as 'maladjusted' although there is no clear-cut distinction between disruptive and maladjusted pupils. Rather their behaviour falls at different points along a continuum and it is a subjective decision as to where the line is drawn between the two.

How is disruptive behaviour identified and measured?

It is obvious that there can be no simple formulae or procedures for identifying and measuring disruptive behaviour. Clearly some acts of misbehaviour are trivial and form part of the general school experience of most pupils. Others, however, are serious and may disrupt classroom life. Unfortunately, it is not always easy to distinguish between the two kinds of behaviour. Thus, even an act as trivial as not having a pen or pencil, or the right equipment for a particular activity, may represent a calculated act of defiance on the part of a pupil and have an effect on both teacher and class far exceeding the overt seriousness of the act. Furthermore, the perceived strength of the misbehaviour may stem not from any particular act, but rather from the accumulation of many relatively trivial incidents which may result in a 'flashpoint' reaction from an exasperated teacher.

In school, disruptive behaviour is generally identified in a non-quantitative manner by teachers and its measurement is thus random and subject to bias. This is illustrated by Wigley (1980) who in the course of an in-service training course asked teachers to identify pupil misbehaviour and keep a record of its frequency. She found that in several cases the offending behaviour actually occurred less often than the teacher had supposed. Furthermore this was sometimes no more frequent with the target pupil than with other pupils in the class who were perceived by the teachers as being quite well-behaved.

Researchers have made a number of attempts to quantify behaviour by means of rating scales. These scales have been extensively used in various surveys and are also used to screen large groups, in order to identify any pupils who need special help. However, such scales are seldom used routinely by teachers, although they could be, since they are easily available. They usually consist of checklists of misbehaviours which teachers rate as being the frequent or infrequent actions of a particular pupil.

Perhaps the most commonly used of these scales is the Rutter 'B' scale developed by Michael Rutter (1970). The scale consists of 26 statements about a pupil (for example, 'Is often disobedient' or 'Often tells lies'). The teacher has to indicate whether the statement applies, applies somewhat, or

3

does not apply to the child in question. The scale has been used by Rutter and colleagues in their study of ten year olds living on the Isle of Wight and in an Inner London Borough (1975).

Another frequently used behaviour scale is the Bristol Social Adjustment Guide. A series of statements about children's behaviour are presented to the assessor who then underlines those statements most applicable to the child being assessed.

A rather different type of behaviour scale has been developed by colleagues in the Research and Statistics Branch of the ILEA. This scale allows teachers to make positive as well as negative ratings on a number of different dimensions of adjustment to school, such as learning skills and learning problems, self-confidence and anxiety, and co-operative or aggressive behaviour (Kysel and Varlaam, 1983).

Behaviour scales can be useful, but they have two major disadvantages. First, like the child-focused definitions we discussed earlier, they treat misbehaviour as if it were the sole responsibility of the pupil. Thus, they can be (potentially) useful in identifying children who are prone to misbehaviour, children who misbehave regularly (and children who have some personality disorder), but they are rather unreliable and poor instruments for identifying and measuring the extent and nature of disruptive behaviour within a school or classroom. Second, behaviour scales on individual pupils can take no account of the relationship between pupil and teacher. Such scales are completed about pupils by teachers, never the reverse! A teacher who has difficulty in keeping control of a class is obviously more likely to identify misbehaviour than is a colleague with better classroom management skills. Thus, although useful for some purposes, behaviour scales are not very suitable instruments for the sensitive identification of misbehaviour.

Observation by school inspectors or trained researchers using specially designed schedules presents a more useful technique. It is, however, an expensive tool and tends to be used sparingly. The amount of time given to classroom observation by HMI in their study of secondary schools was very limited. Similarly, in research studies of primary schools (Galton et al., 1980) and secondary schools (Rutter et al., 1979) the amount of time used for observation for any one class was limited.

Have standards of behaviour changed over the past decades and how widespread is disruptive behaviour today?

Despite the coverage given to the topic of disruptive behaviour by the popular press, the evidence on whether standards of behaviour in schools have changed is both limited and unreliable. This is partly because, as already noted, the identification and measurement of misbehaviour is not easy, and partly because a disruptive incident in 1960 may not have the same potential for disruption in 1983. Some may argue that this is, itself, proof that standards have deteriorated, but this may not be necessarily true. Certainly schools have changed, just as life in general has changed. Society is less conformist, better informed and, in many instances, more affluent than it was in 1960. However, the unemployment figures over the past decade indicate that, for some, the affluence of the 1960s has not lasted and, for many younger people, it has hardly been experienced.

Changes in the attitudes of pupils, their parents and in society in general, are likely to affect views on how pupils should behave in schools. Twenty years ago, in most schools, pupils would stand up when an adult entered a classroom and they would punctuate the answer to every question with 'Miss' or 'Sir'. Today many pupils do neither. This is not due to any lack of respect for their teachers but rather because schools have become less formal and this change has affected adults' attitudes as much as those of pupils. Many visitors to schools would prefer to see pupils absorbed in a task rather than being distracted by having to give formal greetings to every visitor, and many teachers would find the constant interjection of 'Miss' or 'Sir' an irritating distraction from the work in hand.

This change in the style of schools makes the question of whether there has been a decline in the standards of pupil behaviour very difficult to answer. That pupil behaviour has worsened – and that it is likely to deteriorate further – is part of educational folk-wisdom. Some writers, such as Jones-Davies (1976), not only maintain 'that a significant deterioration in the behaviour of children in secondary school appears to be beyond dispute' but talk of 'the significant acceleration in the incidence of disruptive behaviour and the increasing inability of some schools to manage such

5

problems'. Not enough reliable statistical evidence exists, however, to support this view. This is partly because many headteachers and teachers, not wishing to appear incompetent, are reluctant to admit that they have behaviour problems in their schools. One result of this reticence is that surveys aimed at gathering such information frequently suffer such a low response rate that their findings are of little more than anecdotal value. For example, a survey carried out by Lowenstein (1972) produced a response rate of only 18 per cent from secondary teachers - and only 5 per cent from primary teachers.

A much higher response rate has been achieved in the various stages of the longitudinal National Child Development Study (NCDS) carried out by the National Children's Bureau (NCB). This research has charted the development of all children born during one week in March 1958. The children have been studied at birth, 7, 11 and 16 years. At the age of 7 teachers assessed the children using the Bristol Social Adjustment Guide (BSAG). The results showed that teachers considered 22 per cent of the children to be 'unsettled' and 14 per cent of them to be 'maladjusted'. In the 16-year old follow up, the Rutter 'B' scale was used in preference to the BSAG. In presenting the findings on the 16-year olds Fogelman (1976) reports that statements like 'open disobedience' referred to some 18 per cent of pupils and 'irritable' to 20 per cent of pupils. However, since different means of assessment were used on the two occasions the results are not strictly comparable.

When Rutter et al. (1970) investigated the incidence of educational and psychiatric disorders among 10-year olds on the Isle of Wight and in an Inner London Borough, they found that both sorts of problems were twice as common in the inner city area as on the Isle of Wight. These data were collected in the 1960s and there is no comparable recent study alongside which to set them.

Surveys carried out by the DES have produced estimates of the number of disruptive incidents occurring in a school, but, as no previous surveys using the same definitions of disruption have been carried out, it was not possible for the DES to ascertain whether there had been an increase in the number of incidents in recent years. Whilst several surveys have confirmed an increase in general teenage misbehaviour in America, various research studies have failed to produce similar evidence in England and Rutter (1979), after an extensive review of the literature on adolescence, concluded that: 'It is clear that the general pattern of adolescent development and disorder has not altered to any substantial extent in recent years'.

It is possible, however, to present some evidence on the current prevalence of disruptive behaviour in schools, although this, too, has to be treated with caution. The HMI Inspectorate survey of a 10 per cent sample of secondary schools found that 'most teachers and pupils alike work hard and have some solid achievement to show' (DES, 1979). HMI Eric Bolton, commenting on the Inspectorate's sub-sample of 18 schools in catchment areas with major social and economic difficulties, argues that 'it is clear from the evidence that the vast majority of schools are orderly places and that most pupils are as well-behaved as they ever were. It would be quite wrong to depict schools as blackboard jungles where teachers are facing violent, rebellious, sullen adolescents in an uneasy and unproductive confrontation. It cannot be claimed that the generality of secondary schools are experiencing major conflict between teachers and taught. Even in schools which are likely to face greater difficulties than most, there is little to support the idea of a major breakdown in order and discipline' (Bolton, 1981).

Factors associated with disruptive behaviour

Whilst it is not possible to claim that factors in a pupil's family or school environment directly cause misbehaviour, there are certain aspects of family and school experience which are clearly associated with disturbed or disturbing behaviour in school.

Parental Influence Part of the context of pupils' school behaviour must be the home background of the pupil and the attitudes of parents to their children's behaviour. There is considerable evidence to suggest that early childhood experiences affect children's subsequent development, although unhappy experiences are no longer considered to be irreversibly damaging (Clarke & Clarke, 1974). There seems little doubt that 'parents help shape the child's behaviour by means of their selective encouragement and discouragement of particular behaviours, by their discipline and by the amount of freedom which they allow' (Rutter, 1975). Inconsistent discipline - punishing a behaviour one day whilst overlooking the same behaviour the next day, or one parent being lax and the other being harsh - seems to have a negative effect.

The timing and quality of parents' responses also help shape good or bad behaviour. Much misbehaviour is attention-seeking and if that is the only way in which a child can gain adult attention he or she is likely to persist in the undesirable behaviour. Rutter claims that, quite early on, the parents of troubled children 'begin to differ from other parents in being less good at recognising when and how to intervene, in giving less encouragement and praise for good behaviour, in responding erratically and inconsistently to bad behaviour and in giving a lot of attention (both positive and negative) when the child is misbehaving' (1975). It is, however, not hard to understand the 'let sleeping dogs lie' approach when a frequently naughty child is being good. Parents may well have more pressing matters to occupy them than that of praising good behaviour, however desirable and ultimately beneficial it may be.

In their comparative study of the Isle of Wight and an Inner London Borough, Rutter and colleagues found that parents in the inner city suffered from more social disadvantages; worse housing conditions; more family discord; more mental disorder and more criminality. Their children were twice as likely to have emotional, behavioural and reading problems as their counterparts on the Isle of Wight. About 1 in 7 ten-year olds in their sample were not living with their natural parents and 'a broken home' was associated with delinquency and child psychiatric disorder. Claims that children living in one-parent families are more likely to be disturbed and disturbing have, however, to be treated with caution since family disruption is frequently associated with longer-term social and economic adversity. Evidence from the NCD Study (Davie et al., 1972) and from our own work in the ILEA has shown that children from single-parent homes are no different from those from two-parent families once allowance has been made for economic factors. Associations similar to those found by Rutter, between home and other background variables, and behaviour and reading attainment were also reported in the ILEA Literacy Survey (Varlaam, 1974).

Finally, the Report of the Committee on Child Health Services (the Court Committee, 1976) concluded that 'there is now extensive evidence that an adverse family and social environment can retard physical, emotional and intellectual growth . . . and adversely affect educational achievement and personal behaviour.'

However, despite such evidence, from these and other similar surveys, it is difficult to find evidence to relate directly, specific classroom incidents to situations external to the school. Research has little to offer on this topic. Quite properly, pupils' individual home lives are seen as distinct from school activity. Unless the pupils link the two aspects of their life, no-one is able to piece the two together though teachers and researchers (as we have shown above) frequently invoke explanations of home or neighbourhood difficulties in seeking the cause of school behaviour problems.

Taking part in classroom activities is likely to be difficult for pupils whose home life is in any way unsettled. If, for instance, parents are experiencing great stress, perhaps as a result of unemployment, poverty or poor housing, this may have severe consequences for the behaviour of their children in school. Low income may mean that parents have to spend more time at their job or on household tasks which leaves them less time to attend to the needs of their children. Parental stress picked up by children may make concentration difficult. Poor housing conditions may mean inadequate sleep, lack of privacy in which to do homework, which in turn could affect concentration, behaviour and attainment. Where a parent or sibling is seriously ill the demands of school must come second to those of home. Some pupils may attempt to cope with difficult situations by 'acting out' in an aggressive fashion or by demanding attention of the teacher or fellow pupils. For others, however, the reaction may be to withdraw. In this case, misbehaviour as such is less common, though full participation in classroom life cannot be expected.

The number of pupils whose home life is unsettled, at least temporarily, is likely to increase. Despite the improvements in child health that have been recorded this century, the psychological pressures on pupils have undoubtedly grown, due, in part, to the increase in divorce –

often preceded by a long period of acrimony - and to the effects of the current economic recession.

Peer Group Influence A child's relationships with other children are important from quite early on since persistent disturbed relationships are an indication that something is wrong with the child's psychological development. According to Rutter: 'Children who are socially isolated or rejected by other children are considerably more likely than other children to have psychiatric problems' (Rutter, 1975). As children grow older their peer group becomes an increasingly important influence on their behaviour. The influence of the peer group on teenagers is particularly strong and may form a 'counter culture' within the school. Hargreaves (1967) and Lacey (1970) have both described the process of peer-polarisation which can result in the forming of an anti-school group which only likes those teachers who allow them the freedom to 'have a muck-about'. Similarly, Willis (1977) has described how the working-class boys in his study formed peer groups which manifested 'entrenched general and personalised opposition to authority' and attached the greatest importance to 'having a laff!'.

School Influence Schools are social institutions and, as such, operate on a basis of rules being accepted by pupils and teachers. Within the school, teachers are accorded more power than pupils, although, obviously, there are many more pupils than teachers. If harmonious relations are not achieved, rules may not be accepted. In these circumstances misbehaviour can reach serious levels and become the accepted norm for the majority of pupils. Without the incentive for pupils which can be provided by the expectation of examination success, teachers may find it difficult to establish the norm of good behaviour. This is the kind of situation described by Reynolds (1975). He argues that, in schools where academic success is rare, teachers and pupils make a truce. In return for behaviour which avoids the worst excesses, teachers agree not to 'hassle' pupils. Thus little homework is set and classroom demands are moderate; uniform, where it is supposed to be worn, is not insisted upon and a fairly lax atmosphere is tolerated.
Reynolds' ideas are speculative; no clear evidence exists to support such a view. These

ideas do, however, relate directly the collective behaviour of pupils to the prevailing ethos of the school. A similar view has been put forward by Rutter and his colleagues in their study of twelve secondary schools (Rutter et al., 1979). Both these views see behaviour and the general state of the school as interdependent. This is a radically different viewpoint from those who see individual pupils as bearing the sole responsibility for misbehaviour. It is a view, however, which complicates any understanding of such behaviour. In addition to the need to view a disruptive act as part of the interaction between pupil and teacher, it is also necessary to view it within the context of the school.

Perhaps some of the variation in teacher-reported behaviour patterns and rates between schools reported in studies of school differences and school effectiveness, are more apparent than real in that, for example, actions perceived as misbehaviour by one teacher (or a set of teachers in a particular school) may not be viewed in the same way by other teachers. As Jones-Davies and Cane (1976) put it: 'One man's disruption may approximate to another's peak teaching experience'. Furthermore, teachers, like parents, can be inconsistent and accept behaviour from one pupil that they would not accept from a different pupil or from the same pupil on a 'bad' day. Again, research has found that some schools also reject behaviour which others will tolerate (Galloway, 1976). These differences in teacher-toleration have been related to specific classroom management skills (Kounin, 1970). What teachers report as disruptive behaviour may, therefore, vary and differ from day to day, class to class, and school to school. Nevertheless, when allowances are made for such variation as there is in teachers' perception and reporting of disruptive behaviour, substantial differences remain between schools in behaviour patterns and rates.

Some of this variation may be explicable in terms of teacher expectations. Much has been written by sociologists of education on the phenomenon of teacher expectations and the self-fulfilling prophecy by which teachers treat pupils in ways likely to make their expectations come true. For example, Hargreaves (1967) has described what he calls stages of speculation, elaboration and stabilisation. That is, the teacher makes tentative guesses (speculation) based on first impressions, of what kind of pupil a newcomer is and is going to be. The teacher then seeks confirmation (elaboration) of these views (perhaps from past schools' reports, and other teachers' views). By taking note of anything which confirms his or her views - by selectively noting supporting evidence - he or she establishes a stereotyped view of the pupil (stablisation) which categorises the pupil in the teacher's mind.

This model of Hargreaves' is interesting but leaves aside the vital question of how the negative (or indeed the positive) views of the teacher actually affect the pupil's behaviour. Further research is needed in order to identify the mechanisms that are assumed to be at work. These may be partly psychological (most of us find it harder to perform well when someone in authority indicates his low opinion of and expectation for us) - and partly managerial: if teachers, who have lower expectations for some pupils in their groups, actually give less attention to them or are more critical of them, it is easy to see how these pupils may become frustrated and resentful.

Clearly, much classroom behaviour is influenced by the general atmosphere of the class. Anyone who has brought up a family knows that it is difficult to prevent children squabbling. With a full class of pupils the difficulty is amplified. Considerable skill is needed in order to structure the class so that large numbers of young people can live together harmoniously and engage in worthwhile learning. Given that some of these pupils will be victims of acute social disadvantage and of difficult home conditions, super-human teaching qualities may be necessary. That said, it is clear that most teachers are able to organise classes so that disruptive behaviour is reduced to an acceptably low level.

In short, behaviour in the classroom is the product of many different factors. These include the personality, temperament and motivation of the pupil; the effects of parents, home and neighbourhood; the influence of the pupil's friends; the collective attitude of the class; the classroom skills of the teacher; and the ethos of the school.

How is disruptive behaviour dealt with?
There are a number of different methods of dealing with disruptive behaviour. Some teachers believe that the most effective of these, paradoxically, is

to ignore it. This view is based on behaviourist theory and relies on the lack of positive attention being a sufficient punishment. Critical to the success of this approach is the need for the teacher to reward good behaviour. Such an approach many seem to be no more than common sense yet it is surprising how frequently teachers forget to do this (Rutter et al., 1979).

Sometimes disruptive behaviour is 'managed' rather than dealt with. Many secondary schools have embraced the concept of pastoral care and teachers with this responsibility endeavour to manage the behaviour of their pupils by, for example, counselling. Their task is not simple for they have to combine the role of friend and adviser to pupils in difficulty, with that of disciplinarian to those whom they view as culpable. Deciding which role is the more appropriate is not always easy. The pastoral care staff have to find the correct balance between the two roles.

In some secondary schools a non-teaching counsellor is employed in order to provide help and guidance to individual pupils. Where this is the case the role of the other pastoral care staff is less ambiguous, but, even so, such appointments are not always welcomed. Teachers, too, have needs and some do not like being the disciplinarian without also being the confidante. Various HMI reports have noted that pastoral care staff are generally successful in their task of managing misbehaviour (HMI, 1978). It is certainly a credit to these workers that misbehaviour is kept in check in so many schools.

One recent experiment has been the establishment of support teams made up of teachers and psychologists. These teams work in ordinary schools and aim to help teachers to cope with disruptive pupil behaviour. Their role - which includes observation of lessons as well as working individually with pupils and teachers - inevitably takes them into a field of ongoing in-service work. Preliminary results from a self-evaluation study of one such experimental team are encouraging (Coulby & Harper, 1981).

Where disruptive behaviour appears to be related to home circumstances (and especially when truancy or condoned absence is common) the Education Welfare Service (EWS) is involved. Educational welfare officers (EWOs) are trained in social work methods and liaise between home and school. Unfortunately, they often carry enormous case loads and, as a result, can concentrate only on the most serious cases. Frequently, this permits them to deal only with pupils attending court or those in crisis circumstances.

An additional method of dealing with disruptive behaviour is to punish it. There are, of course, a number of different types of punishment that can be inflicted. Traditional forms are the giving of lines to write out or learn, and the detaining of pupils after school hours. Within a class, teachers sometimes resort to such tactics as making pupils stand up, sending them out of the room, or telling them off, either in private, or in the hearing of the whole class. However, for pupils intent on serious disruption, lines and detention are only a slight deterrent and a public 'telling off' may well give them the attention they are really seeking.

Another traditional form of punishment is caning. In recent years corporal punishment has become a highly controversial issue - both on legal and educational grounds. Since 1982 (when the Republic of Eire banned corporal punishment) Britain has been the only European country in which teachers cane pupils. At the same time (1982) the European Court of Human Rights declared that corporal punishment violated the European Convention on Human Rights to which Britain is a party. The Court judged that parents had the right to forbid the caning of their children. Although several LEAs have now banned the use of corporal punishment, in many it remains a possible sanction, its use, being governed by strict regulations, involving the keeping of records in a 'punishment book'. However, the Government has recently indicated that parents may stipulate that they do not want corporal punishment used on their child. Its use is thus likely to be reduced further in the coming years.

Corporal punishment, although used for many years, does not appear to be very effective. The research findings of Rutter and colleagues showed very different levels of corporal punishment between schools, yet also showed that these levels were related neither to the standards of behaviour within the school nor to the individual behaviour of pupils in their previous primary school (Rutter et al., 1979).

Suspension (not allowing a pupil to attend school for a limited period of time) and expulsion (permanently excluding a pupil from a particular school) are additional means of dealing with serious disruptive behaviour. Like corporal punishment, both suspension and expulsion are subject to the regulations of the LEA. In some authorities, these regulations have been revised recently and now include the opportunity for parents to appeal against the punishment of their child (ACE, 1982). Although this particular type of parental involvement occurs at a time of crisis, it is only fair to note that many teachers involve parents at earlier stages. In some schools, for instance, it is common for weekly reports to be sent to the home of any pupil whose behaviour is causing concern. Likewise, parents are often asked to meet staff in order to discuss the behaviour of their children.

Suspension – although ostensibly providing an immediate solution to the problem by removing the pupil – is of questionable value for it may destroy what little remains of a pupil's commitment to school. Suspension may also place the individual at risk by denying him or her the security of somewhere safe to go each day, and of a daily school routine.

For pupils who are persistently disruptive a further possibility is referral to special education. This is normally on the recommendation of an educational psychologist. Schools for the 'maladjusted' specialise in pupils with serious behaviour problems. However, there are only a very small number of places in maladjusted schools. (Approximately 9,000 in England and Wales which amounts to provision for 0.1 per cent of the pupil population.)

Whilst referral to special education is of considerable benefit to some pupils, for others, the compensation of having their behaviour tolerated and skilled guidance provided, may be negated by the removal from ordinary school and, in some cases, by the dispatch to boarding schools some distance from home.

Another possible method of dealing with pupils who are persistently disruptive is to remove them from the ordinary classroom yet neither suspend them, nor send them to special schools. Of course, this has always been a safety valve for a harassed teacher who has resorted to sending a pupil out of class in order to provide relief for both teacher and pupil and to permit a 'cooling-off' period. Recently, though, what was viewed as a temporary solution has been extended in various ways. The result is that there now exist several different kinds of provision for the withdrawal of pupils from ordinary classes. Tattum (1982) lists no fewer than fifteen types of unit with educative, therapeutic, diagnostic, clinical or disciplinary goals. The broad title for these units is support centres. The aims, facilities and methods of these units are discussed in some detail by Tattum.

Given a system of formal schooling such as exists in most Western countries, disruptive behaviour is unlikely to disappear. Conflict between pupils, or between teachers and pupils, is bound to arise. What appears crucial to us is for schools to be organised so that such behaviour is reduced and its disruptive effects are kept to a minimum. Both pupils and teachers have the right to dignity and, just as a bullying sarcastic teacher is an abuse of authority, so no teacher should have to tolerate constant goading and ridicule.

For schools to be successful some balance has to be found between the needs and rights of pupils and those of their teachers. At best this can result in a school where pupils and staff co-operate in a joint approach to learning and where, notwithstanding any isolated incident, the general atmosphere is harmonious. At the secondary level, if a school is academically successful and pupils achieve well in public examinations and go on to employment, or further (or higher) education, then the creation of such an atmosphere - although far from inevitable - may be relatively easy. If, however, the secondary school is not academically successful even though the teachers are competent - perhaps because the intake of pupils to the school is extremely disadvantaged - then, quite obviously, the task facing the teachers is much more difficult.

Before ending this chapter and going on to discuss our study of support centres, we wish to make three further points about behaviour in school. First, from the teacher's point of view, the skill needed to co-ordinate and teach a large class of pupils and ensure that each individual can learn effectively, is substantial. Second, the structure of school organisation means that the needs of individuals have to be secondary to the needs of the class, which inevitably makes pupil conformity a valued objective. Third, there are few other instances of similarly organised situations in which a majority have to conform to strict rules, whilst an individual retains total control. In these circumstances, as Kyriacou and colleagues (1978) have demonstrated, the stress for teachers can be considerable and the pressure on pupils (as Raven (1979) and others have argued) can also be unbearable.

Summary
This chapter has attempted to answer several questions concerning disruptive behaviour in schools. The difficulties surrounding definitions and perceptions of such behaviour have been noted – as has the lack of conclusive evidence on changing standards of behaviour. The contribution of family and peer influences on disruptive behaviour have been described and the importance of viewing misbehaviour not in isolation but in the context of the school has been stressed. The links between these broader social factors are complex, and our knowledge about them is often no more than speculative and necessarily inconclusive. Treatment of disruptive behaviour is more straightforward although not necessarily more successssful.

Chapter 2

WHAT ARE SUPPORT CENTRES?

'Support Centres' is one of the terms used to describe the special provision - catering largely for pupils with behaviour problems - that, in recent years, has developed outside both ordinary and special schools. Other names given to centres are 'disruptive units' and 'behavioural units'. A more emotive term sometimes adopted by the media is 'sin bin'.

Centres have developed in a variety of different ways. Some are merely extensions of the ordinary school and are on-site, staffed by regular teachers, and in which pupils mix with their peers at break and lunchtime or attend on a part-time basis. Others are more independent. These are frequently sited away from the main school buildings, they take pupils from several different schools, the staff are appointed directly to the centre and return of pupils to school on a part-time basis is less frequent.

A further distinction is that some centres are run by voluntary agencies and merely supported by grants paid by the LEA. Naturally in these cases the particular emphasis of the voluntary agency is often reflected in the type of centre that is operated. (Thus many such centres have been set up to cope primarily with pupils with attendance problems rather than those showing disruptive behaviour.) In addition there are a number of intermediate treatment centres set up for pupils 'at risk' and run by social services departments. Finally, in some LEAs, educational guidance centres, which are supervised by the schools psychological service, are also included within the general category 'support centre'.

This range of alternative provision presents a somewhat bewildering array in contrast to the uniformity of most secondary schools. They represent a distinct educational movement very different from well established special education with its medical and treatment emphasis. As Tattum (1982) has pointed out, their growth has coincided with the acceptance of the general Warnock principle of the integration of handicapped children into ordinary schools. It is ironic, therefore, that these two developments should have occurred at the same time and yet point in such different directions: Warnock to integration, support centres to differentiation.

How did the idea of support centres gain ground?

Background
There were several pressures and influences which can be seen to have had some bearing on the development of support centre policies. Some of these influences came from changes in laws relating to children, and from national educational debates; others stemmed from social, demographic and organisational changes and from the growth of lobby groups for specific issues. (These influences are discussed in detail in Payne, 1980.)

As far back as 1969 the passing of the Children and Young Person's Act had abolished remand homes and approved schools. The result was that young people could no longer be placed in residential institutions for lengthy periods and heads of community homes could refuse to admit young people whom they considered might be particularly difficult. The burden of provision for these young people was placed on LEAs. Moreover, with the raising of the school leaving age to 16 in 1973 there were more older pupils in school - not all of whom revelled in the prospect of an extra year's education.

The Labour Government of 1974-79 introduced changes in the Rate Support Grant which favoured inner city authorities and this, together with the Urban Aid programme, made more money available for educational projects. The same government launched the 'Great Debate' following James Callaghan's speech at Ruskin College, Oxford, in October 1976 in which concern was expressed at the inability of the education system to maintain standards of work and behaviour. Payne suggests that attention may thus have been drawn 'to those features of schools

19

which resulted in loss of teaching time to the average child'.

At local level, the early 1970s were a time of teacher shortage and rapid teacher-turnover in secondary schools. Industrial disputes led to part-time schooling for some children (Rutter et al., 1979). Many urban authorities had a turnover rate nearly twice as high as the rest of the country (see Little, 1977). The difficulty of retaining experienced teachers is illustrated by an ILEA survey, noted by Little, in which it was found that 77 per cent of men and 87 per cent of women had been teaching in their school for less than five years. Many schools, therefore, were faced with the joint problems of high staff turnover and a high proportion of inexperienced teachers.

Demographic changes in many metropolitan areas - a combination of slum clearance and 'middle income flight' (Thornbury, 1978) - together with housing renewal and 'gentrification' (Briault, 1975), widened the gap between socio-economic groups in the catchment areas of some inner city schools. During these years the 'alternative' education movement gained ground with the opening of several alternative institutions many of which were run by voluntary groups and regarded with toleration by LEAs.

Corporal punishment was abolished in primary schools in some LEAs during the early 1970s and the Society of Teachers Opposed to Physical Punishment (STOPP) is committed to campaign for a complete ban. This campaign may well have increased teacher pressure for alternative sanctions or more teacher support in dealing with difficult pupils.

Finally, the abandonment of the 11+ selection examination and the incorporation of grammar schools into a comprehensive system may have had an effect on the setting up of centres. Newsam (1979), for example, claims that reorganisation influenced the development of the ILEA's policy on disruptive pupils. Parents whose children, under the former system, might have attended grammar schools, stressed that they would not tolerate their children's educational opportunities being damaged by time lost in school disruption.

Local authority interest in, and the growth of special units during the 1970s as a means of coping with pupils with behaviour problems has been described by Young, Lawrence and Steed (1980) in their detailed analysis of documents sent to them by 49 LEAs in England and Wales. Both Young et al.

and Berger & Mitchell (1978) claim that in those LEAs where heads and teachers formed a majority on LEA 'disruption' working parties, the setting up of units was much more likely. According to these writers, where heads and teachers were in a minority, a broader approach which included some critical consideration of the curriculum, improving in-service training and increasing the number of educational psychologists and special education advisers, was adopted.

Thus a number of different factors contributed to the development of support centres. In many ways extending provision for pupils with behaviour problems can be seen as similar to setting up special maladjusted schools. However, many teachers are critical of the notion that pupils who disrupt their own learning are necessarily 'maladjusted'. Furthermore, there had long been a feeling amongst teachers that special educational placement - controlled either by school doctors or educational psychologists - was too rigid. What was needed was a more flexible provision which pupils could move in and out of and which would have neither the effect of labelling pupils as deviant nor the delays and separateness of a system of special education.

Extent of Support Units

The DES did not set in train any major initiative on disruption in school until the late 1970s - perhaps out of a feeling that it was an issue best dealt with by the LEAs, or perhaps because it was felt that publicity would serve merely to enhance and increase the incidence of disruptive behaviour. However, at a conference in 1976 the Secretary of State promised that HMI would collect information on disruptive pupils in special units associated with ordinary schools. Thus, the first major survey of support centres (or behavioural units) was carried out by HMI and published in 1978.

The survey was conducted in two stages. In the first stage a letter and questionnaire was sent by HMI to all LEAs in England. A total of 239 units were identified in 69 LEAs. In the second stage a team of eight HMIs visited a sample of almost half the units to assess available facilities and methods.

Two years later the Advisory Centre for Education (ACE) carried out their own survey to find out the number of special units in existence and their distribution, not only in England, but throughout the UK. Of the 84 LEAs which responded to the ACE questionnaire, 59 authorities had a total of 439 units. Thus, two years on from the HMI survey the number of units had grown by 200.

The speedy but piecemeal spread of special units, with little direction from the DES, is reflected in their great diversity of name, objectives and function. Similarly, across local authorities there is considerable variation in the procedures for setting up special units and for their operation and control. Tattum (1982) observes: 'Whilst many LEAs initially approached the problem with reservations, they soon realised the convenience and efficacy of these establishments. Units enable local authorities greater manoeuvrability and flexibility – they can be set up without invoking Section 13 of the 1944 Education Act; they are not required to fulfil the DES's basic school provisions; they enable local authorities to pay salaries outside the negotiated Burnham limits; they can be speedily set up, and should the need arise, equally quickly closed down.'

A number of research studies of support centres have been mounted, though in general, these tend to be small-scale and descriptive rather than evaluative. The rest of this chapter is devoted to a discussion of these studies.

Descriptive Studies of Support Centres

The research that has taken place on support centres has provided a substantial body of information on procedures for referral and return to school, staff and pupil characteristics, the courses offered, and the quality of accommodation.

The research includes the two national surveys, mentioned earlier, carried out by HMI (DES, 1978) and by the Advisory Centre for Education (1980). Additionally, the Schools Council carried out a survey to identify good practice in institutions which included special classes, off-site and on-site units (Dawson, 1980). It should be noted that the samples of centres included in these surveys differed considerably. The HMI survey which was the first to be carried out, encompassed all the LEAs in England, with almost half of the identified centres subsequently being visited by HMI, whereas the ACE survey conducted two years later aimed to collect information on all centres in the UK. However, only just over half of the centres identified returned a completed questionnaire. On the other hand in the Dawson study which commenced shortly after the DES survey and involved all LEAs in England and Wales, the researchers deliberately restricted their interest to any educational establishment where 'good work with disturbed children was going on'.

Other descriptive studies are less extensive and deal with units in only one local authority, for example, Sheffield (Galloway, 1979) and Lancashire (O'Hare, 1980) or with individual or small groups of units (Tattum, 1982; Grunsell, 1978). The findings of these small-scale studies will be dealt with after a discussion of the national surveys under the following eleven questions.

i) Who did centres serve?
In general it is more common for centres to serve several schools than to be linked exclusively with just one institution. For instance, HMI found that whilst a quarter of their sample served only one school, 70 per cent served more than 10 schools each - possibly all the secondary schools in their authority. In the ACE survey (two years later) it was found that 18 per cent of units served 11 or more schools, almost half served between 2 and 10 schools and over a third served only one school. Of the 160 centres or units which provided information in the Schools Council study 38 per cent served the pupils of more than one school, 36 per cent were administered by one school but accepted pupils from other schools and 26 per cent accepted pupils only from the parent school.

ii) What accommodation did centres have?
Almost half the units surveyed by HMI were accommodated in all or part of a disused school or in houses. The rest were sited usually in part of the main school or in huts. But a large group (24 out of 108) were in a miscellaneous assortment of provision, sometimes shared and, predictably in the circumstances, of varying quality. Whilst some of the huts and conversions were praised, there was criticism of dilapidated buildings, low standards of decoration and poor cleaning and sanitation. Each unit had at least one 'classroom', but the availability of space or equipment was variable and on the whole limited. Many units provided art and craft, some had a woodwork bench, cooker or garden which enabled some practical work to be undertaken.

Only eight units had a library or resource centre.
Some shared facilities, often with a wide variety
of other users.

iii) Who were the staff in the centres?

The staff in the units surveyed by HMI had
considerable teaching experience although 20 per
cent were in their early years of teaching and a
few were actually in their probationary year, to
the disquiet of the HMI. The staff in the 27
one-teacher units were, the HMI considered, 'placed
in positions of undue personal and professional
vulnerability'. Many teachers were concerned about
their career prospects from their somewhat marginal
position in the system.

iv) Who were the pupils in the centres?

HMI found that the pupils ranged in age from 4 to
17 years, but by far the largest group (over 50 per
cent of the total) were those from the 4th and 5th
years of secondary schools, that is 14 to 16 year
olds. Overall, 82 per cent of pupils were of
secondary school age. However, the distribution of
ages in some units suggested that some young
children were being educated alongside much older
pupils.

Only 4 per cent of units in the ACE survey
served both junior and secondary pupils. The
majority (68 per cent) served secondary age pupils
and 28 per cent served pupils from 5 to 11. In the
Schools Council Survey, however, 14 per cent of the
units and special classes catered for all ages and
39 per cent were for pupils over ten years of age.
In general, units had more than twice as many boys
as girls.

HMI found that, in most cases, pupils remained
on the roll of their 'parent' school as well as on
the unit's register. Some, however, were only on
the unit's register. Where pupils remained on the
school roll there was a clear link with the school
which may have facilitated the reintegration of the
pupil. As HMI noted 'where no links existed and
children were removed from the school roll, there
seemed a greater possibility of problems of
continuity and of curricular provision'.

ACE claims that 89 per cent of the students in
units remained on the register of their feeder
school but ACE, in contrast to HMI, viewed this
with concern. Whilst HMI saw this system as easing
reintegration, ACE argues that 'referral is largely
seen, therefore, as a 'within institution' change

which, though often causing a drastic change in a
student's circumstances, requires no formal
recognition'.

v) How were pupils admitted to centres?

HMI found that admission procedures in on-site
units usually operated through a committee of
senior staff. Such informal arrangements minimised
the risk of labelling pupils and eased transition
back to mainstream school. In off-site units,
usually serving several schools, the procedures
were more formal and admissions carefully
appraised.

ACE found that less than 40 per cent of the
units (on- or off-site) had separate managing
bodies which handled referrals. Some had an intake
panel which included representatives of the schools
psychological service and local social services.
(In the Schools Council study the psychologist was
used by 80 per cent of all units (on- and
off-site)in the selection of pupils.) Others had
management groups more akin to school governing
bodies. ACE expressed concern, however, that
despite the recommendation in the guidelines on
referral procedures issued by LEAs, there was no
mention of parent representation on the admission
panels or of parent appeals following referral.

vi) What were pupils' attendance rates at centres?

At the HMI-surveyed centres, pupil attendance rates
were high, with off-site centres having an average
rate of 85 per cent and the on-site centres a rate
of 76 per cent. Many of the pupils had poor
records of attendance in their parent school but,
as HMI comment, it is probable that improved
attendance at the centre was the consequence of
closer personal relationships with staff, greater
flexibility and less stringent academic demands.

vii) How long did pupils stay in centres?

In the Schools Council survey Dawson found
variation in the length of time for which pupils
attended special classes or units - the average was
18 months. While most of the pupils in the
autonomous (off-site) units attended for just over
a year, some units had a few pupils who attended
for about three years. On-site units had the
longest average (modal) duration of attendance.

viii) What curriculum was offered in centres?

HMI found the programme of work offered in the units depended on several factors: their overall philosophy; the qualifications and specialisms of their teachers; and the availability of resources. Centres were also found to vary in their philosophical approach. Some had an emphasis on remedial work and sought to enhance basic skills, others aimed at social adjustment and cultural enrichment for their pupils. Many units however, combined elements of all these approaches.

Students in virtually all the centres in the HMI survey studied English and mathematics. History, geography, science, languages and music teaching were far less frequent. Despite this 'half the units claimed they could provide opportunities for pupils to follow external examination courses where desirable'. Sometimes pupils returned to school for particular subjects. Some units drew in staff from the parent schools or offered correspondence examination courses or link courses with nearby FE colleges.

In Dawson's study only English, mathematics and arts and crafts were widely taught and, with PE and one or more of the humanities, made up the 'core curriculum'. In addition to their educational qualities, arts and crafts and PE were considered to have therapeutic value.

ix) Were records of pupil progress kept?

It is obviously of some importance that teachers receive adequate records of the pupils they care for in special units. It is also important that records of work and behaviour be maintained during the time pupils spend in the units.

The HMI survey found that two-thirds of the units received some written record at the time of referral – but a quarter did not. Admittedly some of these would have been on-site units where staff would have access to the usual school files. Once pupils were admitted to the unit most (though not all) staff kept some kind of individual records. HMI stressed the need for systematic and confidential records.

x) Were parents involved in the centres?

HMI found that staff in off-site units made more consistent efforts to encourage parental involvement than did staff in on-site units, which sometimes accepted pupils without consultation with the parents. The question of parental involvement was, not surprisingly, of interest to ACE. In their survey not one of the responding authorities reported the presence of a parent representative on the management body of a centre and their report refers to 'a lack of safeguards to protect the right of students or parents'. Sixty-two per cent of units, even when off-site, did not have separate management bodies and, in those units which did, arrangements varied considerably. Some had an 'intake panel' on which the school welfare and psychological services, as well as local social service departments, were heavily represented. Others had management bodies comprising members of the education committee, head teachers of the schools the unit served, and the teacher-in-charge.

According to the ACE survey, LEA guidelines on referral procedures generally recommended consultation with parents. However, nowhere was there any suggestion that parents or pupils had the option of refusing referral to a unit once headteachers and the officials of the authority had decided on the desirability of such action. Nor were there any instances of appeals procedures being used following referral.

xi) Were there proper procedures for reintegration?
The procedures for reintegration were often less well-developed than those for referral. HMI considered that return to ordinary school was made easier when links with the parent school were well established, but the relative newness of most of the units meant that few had much experience of reintegrating pupils. HMI pointed out that, for the 14 to 16 year olds with a history of disruptive behaviour or chronic difficulties, it was hard to imagine that they would return to school. Long periods in a unit could amount to 'de facto alternative education' with associated problems of financial and curricular provision and, ACE would argue, a threat to democratic rights.

ACE found that 90 per cent of respondent units declared their aim of returning pupils to school although most admitted this was unrealistic, particularly for older pupils in the last two years of compulsory schooling. As already noted, length of attendance varied from a few weeks to two years with one year being the expected length of stay.

Other studies of support centres
Some small-scale studies have been able to look more closely at a few units. David Galloway of

the Education Department of Sheffield investigated behavioural units in the city (Galloway, 1979). Seven schools which had set up a special group for difficult or disturbed pupils were approached. Three schools which had no such group and had no intention of setting one up were also asked to serve as a control group.

The heads of each school were interviewed about their philosophy on pastoral care and discipline and their views on the possible advantages and limitations of special groups. The teachers-in-charge were also interviewed and the researchers spent a week carrying out systematic observation of the special groups. A random sample of teachers throughout the schools was interviewed about discipline and pastoral care in general. Finally a random sample of second and fifth year pupils was interviewed.

The schools in the study varied in size, catchment area and policy. Those schools with special groups had established them in response to different perceived needs and consequently had different emphases; some groups were for younger pupils and some for older pupils. The groups had different philosophies and hence different aims and objectives. All the heads of groups agreed (with one possible exception) that return to ordinary lessons was a central objective. Nevertheless, they disagreed on the appropriate way to achieve this. A form of 'deterrent philosophy' was evident in three of the seven groups; the other groups were orientated more towards treatment and 'constructive social learning'. Moreover, several groups had changed their initial emphasis. 'Without exception, the five groups set up in order to cater primarily or exclusively for deviant, disruptive pupils have either modified or extended their original objectives. Nearly as many children are now admitted to at least one of these groups because they are thought to need counselling and support as because they have been regarded as disruptive'. Galloway suggests that part of the reason for the changing emphasis was the need for teachers to feel they were doing more than 'minding troublesome children'.

In addition to exploring the aims and objectives of the special groups, staffing and facilities were also investigated. The number of pupils was recorded, as was the length of time these pupils attended.

Two schools appeared to be using their special group as a relatively long-term educational alternative, while two others pursued a policy of phased return to ordinary lessons following a fairly short period of full-time attendance. Teacher-pupil ratios were very favourable, although the number of teachers working in each group varied considerably - with consequent effects on the curriculum. In a few groups it was found that the children were working to a somewhat restricted curriculum. Galloway concedes that there may be good reason for this. If pupils have a history of school failure an alternative curriculum with more emphasis on counselling and social learning may be more valuable. However, as Shipman (1980) argues, the longer a pupil remains out of mainstream schooling - particularly if in the meantime she or he is receiving a separate curriculum - the harder will it be to reintegrate. Interestingly, Galloway notes that one problem to emerge was that of establishing a 'close co-operative link' over the curriculum between unit teachers and their colleagues in the school's mainstream. One group had developed specific structures for integrating the group's timetable with ordinary lessons. This group had the highest level of pupil concentration. (However, most of the pupils in the groups showed overall high levels of concentration. This, it was suggested, may have been due to the low pupil-teacher ratio and to the formality of the atmosphere.) Two of the schools had very low rates of corporal punishment; all had clearly developed philosophies on pastoral care and their fifth form pupils were more likely to believe a teacher was interested in them as individuals despite their performance in school work.

Lancashire LEA commissioned O'Hare and colleagues to evaluate the operation of the authority's disruptive pupil units (O'Hare et al., 1980). The first stage of the study was devoted to a familiarisation exercise with a selection of units. Each member of the research team spent one day in at least two of the five centres observing and talking to teachers and pupils. It was decided to employ a combination of questionnaire and interview methodologies. Questionnaires were sent to a variety of the people involved with centres including teachers and parents. Interviews were carried out with headteachers of the parent school of attached and 'semi-detached' centres, with pupils in all the centres in the sample and with the appropriate educational psychologists. Using a case study approach, the research team explored aims and practice, admissions and reintegration, demand for centres and whether they should be attached or detached. Future provision was also discussed.

In brief, the aims of the different centres varied, depending on whether staff saw the major purpose to be rehabilitation or containment. It was found that all the centres suffered because they could not offer a curriculum which would be considered acceptable in normal schools due to the lack of provision of specialist facilities such as laboratories and workshops. As there was no common system of admissions, procedures varied widely. Diversity of intake was considered to exacerbate problems. The report states of one centre 'the impression is gained that the centre has been used as a dumping ground for children who should have been placed elsewhere.'

A powerful first hand description of the trauma and difficulties of reintegrating secondary pupils emerges from Grunsell's (1978) account of his Islington Centre for persistent truants from two London comprehensive schools. The initial aim of the centre was to reintegrate pupils by the end of their first year in the unit. Attempts to maintain links with the two schools were not successful and, after initial disasters, attempts at reintegration were abandoned.

Whilst avoiding grandiloquent claims of 'a miracle cure for young offenders' Grunsell suggests that 'while other kids around them were bundled off into residential institutions ... the centre kids were allowed a breathing space, time to watch, experiment and learn from themselves. Some apparently learned in their time with us. Others ... seemed doomed only to provide a lesson in what not to do.'

Thus a considerable amount of knowledge can be gained by descriptive studies of the work carried out by support centres. More knowledge could, however, be obtained by evaluative studies, though few appear to have been carried out. There are understandable reasons for this shortage of evaluative work. The majority of centres are still very young and many procedures for referral remain experimental. Moreover, there is no way of knowing what the pupils who are referred to the units would have been like had they remained in their own class or parent school. Would their behaviour have worsened or would it, as Topping (1982) speculates, have shown 'spontaneous remission'? Rutter & Graham (1966) have demonstrated that, although some children are troublesome at home and some are troublesome at school, there is little overlap between the two groups. By the same token (and one we explained in the previous chapter), some pupils may be troublesome in some settings - with certain teachers or in certain lessons or peer groups - but not in others.

From the standpoint of scientific rigour it would be helpful, in order to answer such questions, to identify similar matched pairs of pupils who met the referral criteria and randomly to allocate them to either an experimental group (which would receive the 'treatment' of attendance at a support centre) or to a 'control' group which would remain in the school class and receive no special treatment. Apart, however, from the problems of securing the co-operation of teachers (many of whom, as Berg (1980) demonstrates, wish to be rid of troublesome pupils) and of parents, the ethics of such an experiment would be questionable.

However, some limited evaluation is surely necessary if confidence is to be placed in specific interventions. These must have sound theoretical bases and use measurable and educationally relevant criteria. Evaluation of support centres would also appear to be crucial if money is not to be wasted and pupils with problems are not to be further disadvantaged.

Our own study which is reported in the following chapters is an attempt to provide more evaluative material on a sample of centres. Whilst limited by the ethical considerations noted above and, of course, by the high financial costs of detailed observational work, we have gathered data from different sources and attempted to make some evaluation of the work of centres.

Summary
Support centres are a form of special provision catering largely for pupils with behaviour problems. They have developed outside both ordinary and special schools. 'Support centres' (or 'behavioural units') include those sited on school premises ('on-site' centres), those sited away from the main school ('off-site support' centres), together with centres run by voluntary agencies ('voluntary agency' centres), intermediate treatment schemes run by social services

departments and educational guidance centres, supervised by the schools psychological service.

Three large scale studies of support centres have been carried out - by HMI (1978), the Advisory Centre for Education (1980) and the Schools Council (1980). These studies sought to answer a number of questions including: who did centres serve; what accommodation did they have; who staffed the centres; who were the pupils who attended; how were pupils admitted to centres; what were pupils' attendance rates; how long did they stay in centres; what curriculum was offered; whether records of pupils' progress were kept; whether parents were involved in the centres and whether there were procedures for reintegration.

Smaller scale evaluative studies by Galloway (1979) and O'Hare et al. (1980) have looked more closely at the operation of support centres within different LEAs.

A considerable amount of knowledge has been gained by descriptive studies of the work carried out by support centres. However more evaluative research needs to be carried out to discover what the benefits and disadvantages are for pupils attending centres. The study we report is an attempt to provide more evaluative material on a sample of support centres within the ILEA.

Chapter 3

AIMS AND METHODS OF THE RESEARCH

In this chapter we focus on the overall aim of the research and the steps taken in pursuit of it. We also discuss how and why we decided to focus on particular aspects of the study and how we selected the sample of centres, pupils and staff. Lastly, we describe our sources of data and the ways in which the information was collected and analysed.

The overall aim of the research was to conduct a detailed study of a variety of school support centres providing for pupils who, on account of their behaviour, have caused concern in their schools. We decided to concentrate our research effort on three main activities:

1) The collection of information about the pupils and staff who were in the centres.
2) An analysis of how the centres functioned.
3) The identification of views of pupils and staff on the advantages and disadvantages of centres both to the pupils who attend them, and to the schools from which they have been transferred.

Given the complexity of the ILEA School Support Programme we decided that it would be most useful to approach the study from a variety of different viewpoints. Each viewpoint is useful in illuminating certain aspects of the Programme and together they provided a portrait of centre organisation and life. We also decided that it was important to examine the Programme from an historical perspective. We have, therefore, included an analysis of the ways in which centres were originally set up, as well as an examination of their current position.

First, we considered it worth describing in some detail the centres as seen through the eyes of the various groups who were most intimately involved with them. We hoped this would enable us to discover how individual views and experiences differed.

Second, in addition to various individual views of the centres, we sought to identify and describe the organisational structure as perceived by the majority of the participants. This included such topics as management, authority structure, curriculum, teaching methods, support for staff and staff training opportunities. This approach also led to an examination of the ways in which links were established, both between the centres and with the wider community of parents, schools and outside agencies.

Finally, the view of centres held by different participants together with our analysis of the organisation and functioning of the centres led to a consideration of areas of tension and conflict within centres, or between centres and schools, and to the examination of ways in which these were resolved. During the developmental stages of any new programme, greater degrees of conflict and strain obviously exist as attempts are made to establish procedures, and as patterns of behaviour are explored. We, therefore, attempted not only to discern how order was maintained but also to identify the main forces at work within the decision-making processes.

In order to pursue our research, we identified four main groups: pupils who were attending the centres; the teachers, social workers and others involved in the 'educational' component of the centres; external staff providing support, guidance and control; and the heads and teachers in the ordinary schools who were being affected by the School Support Programme. Few other researchers had been fortunate enough to encompass such a wide range of different groups. Usually the teaching staff in centres were used as the prime source of information and other groups were only involved peripherally in the data collection process (e.g., HMI, 1978 and Wilson & Evans, 1980).

The Sample
In order to investigate each centre in sufficient detail it was necessary to limit the number of

centres studied. We decided to focus, therefore,
on centres dealing with pupils of secondary age. A
stratified sample of 33 centres was selected from
the 96 on-site secondary centres, off-site support
centres, voluntary agency centres, intermediate
treatment schemes and educational guidance centres
which were functioning within the ILEA at the end
of the Summer term 1979. The on-site and off-site
support centres were included in the sample roughly
in proportion to their representation in the total
number of centres, while the more uncommon types of
centres were represented by five centres each.(1)
The actual centres taking part in the study were
selected at random from their specific groups. (We
found that although we were not aiming to make the
sample geographically representative, at least two
centres were selected from each of the ILEA
divisions.)

The actual number of centres selected from
each type and the percentages of each type which
were included in the sample may be seen in Table
3.1.

Table 3.1: The Centres in the Sample

Centre	Number of centres in sample	% of all centres in category
On-site secondary	10	33
Off-site support centre	8	32
E.G.C.	5	39
Vol. Agcy. centre	4	21
I.T. scheme	5	46
All	32	33

Collection of Data

The fieldwork was conducted during the academic
years 1979-80 and 1980-81. During the initial
stages of the research we assembled the documents
relevant to the establishment and development of
the School Support Programme as a whole and to the

_____

(1) We were forced to exclude one of the voluntary
agency centres following the resignation of their
only member of staff and the temporary closure of
their educational programme.

individual centres, and we visited the centres to discuss the study and observe them at work. The information and ideas gathered during these preliminary visits influenced our decisions to focus on specific areas of life in the centres and our choice and design of tests, questionnaires and observation techniques. In addition we were, of course, influenced by the results of previous research studies, by our knowledge of the concerns being expressed by other researchers, educationalists and the media, and by our own personal views and interests.

Attainment Tests

Although attainment tests are a widely used source of information in education research projects, few of the previous studies of centres had incorporated test results into their data collection. However, we decided that in order to provide a reasonable description of the pupils' general attainment at the time of their referral to centres, a sample of pupils should be asked to complete, within three weeks of their arrival, a mathematics and an English test. Test results are, of course, very limited. We were aware that they could only provide us with an indication of pupils' basic skills in two areas of the curriculum. Nonetheless, we felt it was important to compare the basic skills of the pupils, and standardised tests were the only way of doing this.

The sample of pupils selected to complete these tests consisted of those who arrived in our sample of centres between the Spring half-term 1980 and the end of the Summer term 1980. Mathematics attainment tests were taken by a total of 308 pupils; English tests were completed by 309 pupils. In five centres the teachers refused to allow any of their pupils to complete the tests, arguing that the tests would either distress the pupils, or would not be a fair representation of the pupils' level of attainment.

Pupil Record Forms

Other research studies of centres had drawn on pupil records. Wilson and Evans (1980), for example, reported that during their visits to centres they had consulted school records in order to obtain the past history of pupils. In the present study, in an attempt to provide a more comprehensive picture of the pupils' familial and social characteristics and their progress and behaviour during their school career, we asked the centre staff to complete a questionnaire on those pupils who were chosen for the tests (whether or not they actually took them). These questionnaires were completed by the staff on the basis of school records and from their personal knowledge of the pupil's background and previous school career. Forms were received for a total of 383 pupils.

Staff Interviews

The central phase of our data collection comprised a series of semi-structured interviews with the staff working at the centres. These included at least one interview (lasting two to three hours) with each of the teachers-in-charge or directors of the centres, and a slightly shorter interview with other teaching staff and intermediate treatment workers. A total of 77 staff (out of a possible 93) were interviewed. Naturally, the researchers also talked informally with the various staff during their visits to the centres. This made it possible to gather more qualitative data and to check some impressions gained during the formal interviews. It also helped us to comprehend more fully the issues which had been raised.

The interviews covered a wide range of topics differing somewhat according to the specific role of the interviewee. All staff interviews included questions about the overall goals and objectives of the centres; the educational programme, teaching methods and organisation; arrangements for maintaining contact with the parent schools and the wider community; the processes whereby pupils were received into centres and either returned to school or prepared for the world of work; and relations with parents. The teachers-in-charge and the directors were also asked about their sources of funding, accommodation, access to facilities, staffing arrangements and the way in which these were designed to operate.

By asking all staff for factual information about the way in which their centres functioned, and about their own views and experiences of the processes, we were able to build up a fairly comprehensive picture of their role. By interviewing most of the staff from each centre we were also able to discover areas where there were common tensions or differences in perceptions.

Finally, all staff interviews included questions relating the interviewees' previous teaching and other work experience, their opportunities for training, their current role and job satisfaction and their career aspirations. This discussion of the impact of the centres on the professional development of the staff and their personal well-being was of particular importance as staff are the major resource in the School Support Programme, and are one of the key determinants of its success or failure.

In addition to the semi-structured interviews, we conducted a series of more open-ended interviews with a variety of professional support staff such as deputy heads, educational psychologists and intermediate treatment co-ordinators. These interviews provided us with a fuller picture of the professional support arrangements for staff and the management structures within the centres. They also enabled us to verify data we had collected from the centre staff.

All the interviews during the central phase of the study were conducted in a separate room, usually at the centre, but occasionally elsewhere. The interviews took place during the Spring and Summer terms of 1980.

Pupil Interviews
During our main phase of data collection at the centres, we were also concerned to obtain opinions from pupils themselves. We wanted to learn about their educational experiences, both past and present. With the exception of the study by Wilson & Evans (1980) this area had been largely ignored by other researchers. We had already had the opportunity to talk informally with centre pupils during our preliminary visits and were aware, therefore, of the topics about which they were most concerned. It was also apparent that the pupils varied considerably in the extent to which they were forthcoming in a group, especially when the centre staff were present. We decided that the most valuable information would be obtained by interviewing, individually, a sample of pupils. As their views also appeared to vary somewhat according to their length of stay at the centres, we decided to include in our sample pupils who were at different stages in their 'centre careers'. The final interview sample comprised, on average, six pupils chosen randomly from those in attendance in each centre. A total of 162 pupils were interviewed. The staff in three centres did not wish us to interview any of their pupils as they thought the interviews might distress the pupils or

interfere with the teaching programme at the centre.

We used a structured interview schedule, but allowed the pupils to elaborate when they were eager to provide us with a fuller description of school and centre life. Although this additional information was not always useful in our comparative analysis of centres, it provided us with rich qualitative data giving a colourful picture of what actually went on and helped us to gain insights into pupils' experiences and reactions to the Programme.

The interview schedule covered a wide range of topics and was designed to elicit information about actual events and also about pupils' views and reactions to these events. The areas covered included the reason for pupils' being referred to the centre; the differences they perceived between centre and school life; the benefits and disadvantages which they believed resulted from their attendance; and their personal interests and career aspirations. As many young people were attending the centres because of their behaviour, we also questioned them about the rules existing in centres, the extent to which they conformed to them, and any sanctions which resulted from non-compliance.

The interviews with pupils were voluntary and they were assured that their replies would be treated confidentially. During our initial visits to the centres some of the pupils had been unsure of the researcher's role and intentions. However, by the time of the interviews during the main phase of the fieldwork, the majority of pupils were less apprehensive and frequently replied enthusiastically when asked to express views about their schooling. A few pupils, nevertheless, remained guarded in their replies throughout their interviews.

Observation
In addition to collecting written records and conducting interviews with staff and pupils at the centre, we also made our own independent observations of the centres. We wanted our own ratings of their organisation and philosophy as well as the overall climate of centre activities and relationships. Again, this was a method of collecting information which few other researchers had been able to employ, though Wilson & Evans (1980) do record that they spent some time during

their one-day visits observing the work in the units.

Throughout our many visits to the centres for preliminary discussions and for more formal interviews we were able to collect a considerable amount of information by means of informal observation. In addition to this informal activity, we asked permission to act more formally as observers during at least two 'educational' sessions at each of the centres. At only one of the centres were staff unwilling for us to attend these sessions because they feared that the presence of researchers would interfere with their teaching programme.

When selecting sessions to be observed, we tried to ensure that the breadth of each centre's educational programme was fairly represented. Thus, for example, in one centre we observed a basic skills session, an arts and crafts afternoon, and two periods of group work in which the behavioural difficulties of pupils were discussed.

These observation periods had two main purposes. We were attempting to make judgments on those aspects of centre life where data from records or interviews were likely to be least adequate, for example, the general tenor of relationships amongst staff, and between staff and pupils, and the overall ethos prevailing in the centres. Our periods of observation also gave us some opportunity to construct and refine our models of management to help describe the ways in which the centres functioned.

Throughout all our visits to the centres we emphasised our independence as researchers and usually refrained from participating in activities. We would have liked to have taken a more participatory role, but chose not to do so, as we thought it unlikely that the amount of participation would have been similar in all centres and, therefore, our observations from different centres would not be comparable. During our more formal observation periods we also tried to be as inconspicuous as possible and to limit our interaction with staff and pupils to avoid influencing unduly their behaviour. We recognise that our mere presence at the centre, however inconspicuous, had some effect on the events which occurred, but, we hope that this effect was relatively similar for all centres and will not invalidate comparisons.

School Questionnaire

Once we had completed our interviews and observation at the centres we turned our attention to gathering information on the effects of the School Support Programme on pupils and staff in ILEA schools. As most of the School Support Programme resources were concentrated on older pupils, we focused our study on secondary schools. During our initial discussions with senior staff in schools, it became obvious that they differed considerably in their experiences and in their perceptions of the Programme. We decided, therefore, that it would be most useful if all ILEA secondary schools were included in the study. Consequently 178 heads were asked to complete a questionnaire at the end of the Autumn term 1980. All 178 questionnaires were returned, but 36 heads reported that they had not used any centres and were, therefore, unable to comment on them. The questionnaire - completed either by the head of the school or by the member of staff nominated by the head as having most experience of the Programme - was in two main parts. In the first section we sought to measure the schools' use of, and demand for, the centres during that Autumn term. In the second part we aimed to collect more qualitative information on the schools' perceptions of the effects of the centres on centre pupils, mainstream teachers, mainstream pupils and school management in general. These four areas were selected following our initial visits to schools and were the topics most frequently stressed by staff during our informal discussions. As the teachers held very specific views on particular centres, the questionnaire also allowed space for the effects of each centre to be described separately. A list of all school support centres in the relevant neighbourhood was also included to remind the teachers to comment on all the centres used. The section of the questionnaire concerned with the schools' views on the centres asked for the heads' own assessments of whether the centres' effects were beneficial or adverse. It also allowed space for some qualification and explanation of these assessments. These further comments were used in our analysis and contributed to our description of the schools' perceptions of centre provision.

In the course of the study we developed and used many different research instruments. Because we tried to obtain information from all the different viewpoints of those concerned with

centres, we ended up with an enormous amount of
data. In our subsequent analysis, however, we
found that data collected from different sources
were generally in close agreement and this greatly
increased our confidence in interpreting and
explaining the complex patterns we found.

Summary
The aim of our research was to conduct an intensive
study of a wide range of ILEA school support
centres. A stratified sample of 33 centres was
selected to represent all centres operating at the
time of the study. The emphasis throughout the
research was on exploring the complexities of the
structures, events and patterns of behaviour in the
centres, through the collection and examination of
both objective and subjective data.

As many as possible of those involved in the
centres - pupils, teachers, social workers,
external support staff and school staff - were
included in the study in order to provide a
comprehensive view. Data were collected from a
wide range of different sources, including records,
attainment tests, pupil and staff interviews,
centre observation and school questionnaires.

Chapter 4

PUPILS IN CENTRES

Introduction
In this and the following three chapters, we shall discuss the major findings of the study. These findings are organised into four main areas concerned with the pupils who attend centres, the teachers who work in them, the organisation of centres and how the centres are viewed by teachers in ordinary schools. The first of these - the pupils who attend centres - is the focus of this chapter.

A number of research studies have described the characteristics of pupils who attend centres (HMI, 1978; Wilson & Evans, 1980). However, the information has tended to be somewhat limited; HMI, for example, looked at the reasons for referral to centres whilst Wilson & Evans looked mainly at educational problems of pupils attending them. Other studies have focused more generally on pupils who have been designated 'maladjusted.' The Isle of Wight study, for instance, explored the educational attainments of such a group of children (Rutter et al., 1970).

In this study we have tried to give a fuller account of the pupils who attend support centres. A wide range of pupil characteristics have been explored including reasons for referral, age, sex, ethnicity, parental occupations and academic performance. These details were obtained from the centre teachers on a sample of 383 pupils who arrived at centres between Spring half term and the end of the Summer term 1980. This information is presented and discussed in the first section of this chapter.

The second section is devoted to pupils' views on three main issues - their relations with school

and peers, their spare time interests and their
views on referral.

The Pupils

i) Reasons for referral

The characteristics of pupils who attend support
centres have been explored by other researchers.
HMI (1978), for instance, found that although most
pupils were placed in units because of disruptive
behaviour in classrooms, many were also there
because of their histories of truancy or school
phobia. Even where all the pupils were said to be
disruptive there was a wide variety of individual
case histories, revealing that disruptive behaviour
was a symptom with many different causes, ranging
from psychiatric disturbance or conflict with a
particular teacher, to temporary difficulties in
family situations. The same study found that units
catering for the secondary age range often had a
preponderance of disaffected 14 to 16 year old
pupils who were unlikely to return to school. A
large proportion of these pupils had, in fact, been
suspended from their schools. Wilson & Evans
(1980) also found that many special classes and
units had a mixed intake of disruptive and other
pupils.

The pupils who attended the support centres in
our study were also there for a variety of reasons.
They were not all there on account of their
disruptive behaviour. The pupils generally fell
into two main groups - they were there either
because they were 'non-attenders' (42 per cent), or
because their behaviour was, in some way,
disruptive (44 per cent). The non-attenders
included not only those who were uninterested in
school and who consequently truanted, but also
those who were afraid of going to school, perhaps
because they were shy, withdrawn or bullied. The
pupils who were in centres on account of their
behaviour, were there mostly because their
behaviour was considered unacceptable in schools.
Teachers' descriptions of such pupils included,
'abusive', 'defiant', 'outrageous', 'disturbed',
'rude' or 'silly'. A small number of pupils were
there as a result of bullying or threatening
behaviour, opposition to school rules or because
they had been involved in violent incidents. Other
pupils were referred because of problems with their
school work, family difficulties or other problems

- including drug-taking and parental disagreement with school staff.

Some pupils combined disruptive behaviour when they were in school with periods of absence. Attendance was said to be a problem - if not the main reason for referral - for over two thirds (68 per cent) of <u>all</u> the pupils.

There were some differences between the kinds of pupils attending particular centres. The majority of pupils at on-site and off-site support centres and educational guidance centres had been referred because of 'disruption'. In contrast, most of those referred to voluntary agency centres and intermediate treatment schemes had been referred because of absenteeism or school refusal (see Figure 4.1).

Figure 4.1: Main Reason for Referral by Centre Type

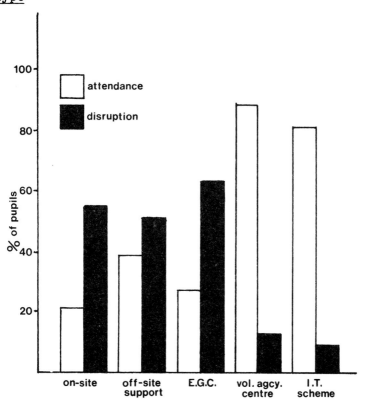

ii) Age
The vast majority of pupils in the centres ranged from 11 to 16 years, as can be seen in Figure 4.2.

Figure 4.2:   Percentage of Pupils of Different Ages

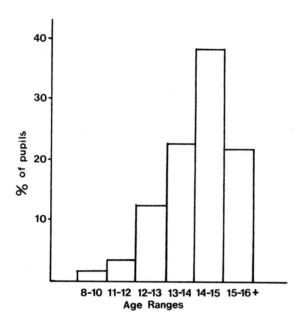

Just over 60 per cent of the pupils were 'older' secondary pupils (14 to 16 years) and just under 40 per cent were in the younger age group of 11 to 13 years. (The few pupils under 11 were attending educational guidance centres.)

On-site centres, educational guidance centres and intermediate treatment schemes, generally took younger pupils, whilst in off-site support centres over two thirds were 'older' secondary pupils. In voluntary agency centres, 93 per cent were in this older age group.

iii) Sex of pupils
Overall there were more boys in the centres (56 per cent) than girls (44 per cent). In all except on-site centres, there were more boys than girls.

In off-site support centres, educational guidance centres and intermediate treatment schemes there were approximately two boys to one girl whilst in voluntary agency centres, girls and boys were equally represented. In the on-site centres, in contrast, girls outnumbered boys (58 per cent, compared with 42 per cent).

iv) Ethnic background
One criticism frequently voiced about centres is that 'a disproportionately large number of students from ethnic minorities' are being referred to them (ACE, 1980). It was with this in mind that we decided to discover whether there was an over-representation of pupils from ethnic minorities in our sample of centres. Information was provided on the ethnic origin of 301 of the 383 pupils. The majority of the centre pupils (65 per cent) were of English, Scottish, Welsh or Irish origin and a fifth were of Caribbean family background. Three per cent of the remaining pupils were of African origin, 5 per cent from 'other European countries', 2 per cent were Asian and 5 per cent had parents from different ethnic groups.

The results of the National Dwelling and Housing Survey (Department of Environment, 1978) provide a baseline measure against which to compare the findings of this study. The comparison of the two samples is shown in Table 4.1.

Table 4.1: Comparison of National Dwelling and Housing Survey and Results from Study (1980, age 11-16)

Ethnic background	Centre sample	NDHS
European	70.4%	72.2%
West Indian/African	22.6%	15.6%
Indian subcontinent	1.7%	3.4%
Other	5.3%	8.8%

This comparison suggests that pupils classified as European were represented in the sample in approximately the same proportion as in the general population for that age range. Pupils classified as West Indian were, however, somewhat over-represented in centres, whereas those classified as coming from 'Indian sub-continent' or 'other' places were somewhat under-represented. However, caution has to be used in interpreting this finding as the NDHS sample included pupils not

47

attending state schools and, therefore, may have not fully reflected the composition of ILEA schools.

v) Family background

We also collected information on whether pupils were living with one or both parents, and on what their parents' occupations were. Over half (57 per cent) of the pupils lived with both parents. Approximately one third (34 per cent) lived with their mothers only. Of the remaining pupils, 4 per cent lived with their fathers only, and 5 per cent lived with other relatives or were 'in care'.

In the ILEA as a whole, only 23 per cent of pupils in secondary schools were living with a single parent or were 'in care', whereas 43 per cent of the pupils in the centre sample were in this situation. There was, therefore, an over-representation in centres of pupils from one-parent families.

Table 4.2 compares the parental occupations of pupils in the centres with those of ILEA secondary pupils as a whole.(1)

Table 4.2: Occupational Categories of Pupils' Parents (excluding those not in work)

Parental occupation	Centre pupils' parents	ILEA secondary school parents
Non-manual	23.2%	30.0%
Skilled manual	26.0%	37.0%
Semi-skilled and unskilled	50.8%	33.0%
	100.0%	100.0%
	(N=181)	(N=11,755)

As can be seen from Table 4.2, pupils with parents in semi-skilled and unskilled occupations were over-represented among centre pupils, while pupils with parents in non-manual or skilled occupations were under-represented. Over a quarter of the pupils' parents were unemployed. This

(1) Collected from EPA data, 1981. 15,860 pupils in sample. Information on parental occupation of 14,017. Of these, 11,755 (84 per cent) were in work.

compares with only 16 per cent of ILEA secondary school parents.

Levels of attainment
Other research has looked at the academic performance of maladjusted children. Yule (1969), for example, reported that 118 out of 2,200 children between 4 and 11 years, surveyed as part of the Isle of Wight study, were assessed as being maladjusted. These children were found to have a lower level of intelligence than those in the control group. They were also found to be severely backward in reading. On average, the group of maladjusted children were 19 months backward in reading accuracy and 17 months backward in reading comprehension, as measured on the Neale Test of Reading Analysis.

The differences in reading ability between the maladjusted children and the control group were not explained by differences in levels of intelligence because, when allowances were made for these, nearly a quarter of the maladjusted children were at least 28 months retarded in reading compared with 5 per cent of the children in the control group. Yule also reported on the differences in reading attainment between 'neurotic' children and those children - mostly boys - who showed evidence of conduct disorder. The neurotic group of children did not differ from the control group in reading attainment, but the 'antisocial' boys had reading attainments significantly lower than the 'neurotic' children and the children in the control group. Yule concluded that poor reading ability was strongly associated with antisocial behaviour.

Laslett (1977) in reviewing previous literature on the subject, stated that although there is little evidence about failure in mathematics, many maladjusted children are, he suggests, seriously retarded in mathematics. Dawson's (1980) research also indicated that many pupils attending support centres had problems with their school work; he reported that 66 per cent of pupils attending special classes or units showed some retardation in school work and some 70 per cent needed remedial help in the basic subjects.

In order to establish the academic ability of pupils attending the centres in our study, we collected information on the groupings (used within the ILEA) at secondary school transfer. In addition, mathematics and reading tests were given to those pupils who entered support centres, in order to get some indication of the pupils' current academic ability. Information was also obtained on the pupils' examination objectives.

Verbal reasoning

Within the ILEA, a verbal reasoning test is administered to pupils in their last year at primary school. The scores are classified into groups - group 1 accounts for the top 25 per cent of pupils, group 2 accounts for the next 50 per cent of pupils and group 3 accounts for the bottom 25 per cent.

Information on the VR groupings was available for only 201 (53 per cent) of the 383 pupils. Almost half of these 201 pupils were in VR group 2 and 41 per cent were in VR group 3; only 9 per cent were in VR group 1. These pupils were, therefore, under-represented in VR group 1 and over-represented in VR group 3 whilst the proportion of VR group 2 pupils (49 per cent) was similar to that for the ILEA as a whole.

As mentioned above, we arranged for reading and mathematics tests to be given to pupils entering centres. We decided to use two tests (1), designed for younger pupils, so as to minimise test-taking anxiety and frustration among pupils unable to cope with more difficult tests.(2)

---

(1) NFER Reading Test SRB; Maths Test LM20 (ILEA 11+ transfer test)
(2) As these tests were standardised for younger pupils only, the interpretation of the results, particularly for the older centre pupils, is difficult.

Reading
Just over 80 per cent (309 out of 383)(1) of the
pupils in the sample took the reading test. The
raw scores from this test are shown in Figure 4.3.

Figure 4.3: Reading Scores

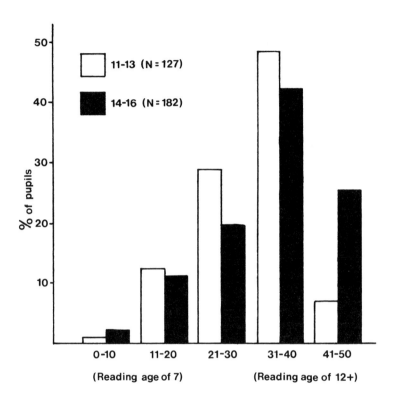

The distribution of scores for the two age
groups was similar, except that (as one might

51

expect) a larger proportion of the 14 to 16 year olds obtained top scores. Nevertheless, most of the 'older' secondary pupils and at least half of the 11 to 13 year olds obtained low reading scores and, in both cases, over 14 per cent had reading ages below 9.

Mathematics

Three hundred and eight pupils took the mathematics test. As no norms or 'maths ages' were available for this test for pupils over 12 years, it was only possible to compare the distribution of centre pupils' scores with that of the scores of ILEA 11 to 12 year olds.

The results are shown in Figure 4.4

Figure 4.4:   Mathematics Scores

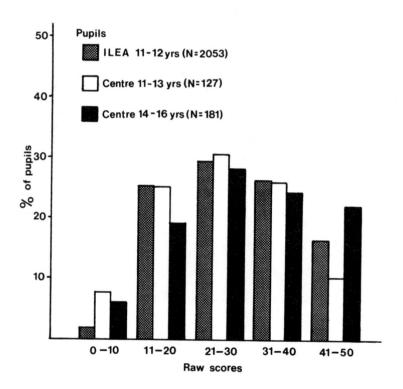

It is clear from this figure that even though no proper norms are available the pupils from centres are attaining less well than their peers in ordinary schools. Older pupils in centres performed better than younger ones, though a number of these performed only at the level of much younger children.

Examinations

Fifty-five per cent of the 'older' secondary school pupils were reported as having examination objectives. The majority of these were preparing for CSE examinations; one was preparing for 'A' level examinations and four for 'O' levels. Eleven pupils were preparing for both 'O' level and CSE examinations.

The information on the 15 to 16 year olds can be compared with the number of public examination entrants in ILEA as a whole. In 1980, 80 per cent of ILEA pupils in this age range were entered for public examinations. In the centre sample, only 46 per cent of these pupils had examination objectives.

Relations with School and Peers

As the two main reasons given for referral were non-attendance at school and disruption within the school, we asked pupils a series of questions about their attendance at school and whether they had got into trouble at school.

Over three-quarters of the pupils interviewed said that they had, at some time, stayed away from school without a reason. Some of these had stayed away occasionally but over half said that they had stayed away regularly for short periods - a few sessions a week or up to two weeks at a time - and over a quarter said they had stayed away from school for longer stretches of over two weeks. A few pupils were non-attenders who had been out of school for several months or even, in one case, for two years. Only a fifth of the pupils said they had never stayed away from school without a reason.

We also asked pupils how they spent their time when they stayed away from school: 41 per cent of the pupils interviewed said that they stayed at home alone, and 4 per cent said that they stayed at home with friends. A fifth of the pupils mentioned going out alone, whilst over a quarter said they went out with a friend. The large number of comments referring to staying at home alone or going out alone (61 per cent altogether) appears to indicate that there were many 'loners' in the sample, as well as the 'classic' truants who prefer the company of the gang or the occasional friend, to going to school.

Finally, we asked the pupils if they had got into trouble at school and whether there were any children with whom they did not get on. Seventy-five per cent of them said that they had 'got into trouble' at school. The reasons most frequently mentioned included 'disruptive behaviour', 'poor teacher relationships', 'violence against other pupils', 'opposition to rules' and 'truancy'. Other reasons included 'violence against teachers', 'theft', 'threatening violence', 'arson' and 'vandalism'.

Almost half of the pupils mentioned more than one reason and some as many as three. It is also worth noting that most of the centre pupils said that their friends also got into trouble at school, mainly for the same reasons as themselves.

Unfortunately, for all the reasons discussed in Chapter 1, reliable information on ordinary school misbehaviour is not readily available, so we cannot say with certainty that the behaviour of this group of pupils is markedly different from that of other pupils in ordinary schools.

When asked about relationships with other pupils, half of those interviewed said that there were pupils they 'didn't get on with'. The majority of these said that there were 'some' pupils they did not get on with, although a quarter said that they did not get on with 'most' of their old school friends. A small number said that there were only 'one or two' children with whom they did not get on.

Nearly half of the pupils said that they used to get into fights. Of these, over a third said they fought 'a lot', over a quarter reported they had occasional fights, whilst a third claimed they had only one or two fights at school. The majority of pupils interviewed denied bullying or having been bullied. Only 3 per cent admitted to having bullied other pupils, whilst as many as a quarter said that they had been bullied or 'picked on'. It is possible that the proportion admitting to bullying is an underestimate due to pupils' unwillingness to own up to such behaviour, but of course, there is no way of knowing that.

From the information gathered from the interviews with pupils and also from the reasons

given by teachers for referral, it is clear that
many of these pupils experienced difficulties in
establishing relationships with teachers and other
pupils, and in conforming to school expectations.
However, only a minority of pupils reported that
they fought with their school mates regularly, or
that they were consistent non-attenders.
Furthermore, very few reported displaying violence
towards teachers.

Pupils views on referral

Pupils in the interview sample were asked a series
of questions in an attempt to discover their
initial reactions to referral. When they first
found out they were going to a centre, over half of
the pupils interviewed claimed that their initial
reactions were positive. Three-quarters of these
pupils focused on the potential of the new
opportunities the centre offered, making such
comments as: 'It was an opportunity to do well'.
Several mentioned the favourable impression they
had gained from their first visit to the centre.
Just over a quarter of those whose initial
reactions were positive made comments suggesting
that they looked forward to referral as providing
'an escape' or change from school: comments
included: 'it was better than school', 'I was glad
to be out of school', and 'I thought you'd have
more freedom'.

Comments made by a fifth of the pupils,
however, implied a negative initial reaction to
referral. Various reasons were given for their
concern. Some pupils were wary of the centre's
reputation and made comments such as: 'I felt
stupid'; and, 'I thought it was a school for
dunces'. Others were concerned about starting in a
new place: 'I didn't know what it was going to be
like'; 'I felt bad'; 'I felt worried'; and, 'I felt
nervous'. Some pupils mentioned the negative
impression they had gained from their first visit;
others were reluctant to leave their school mates.
The remainder of the pupils showed an apparent
indifference to their referral making such comments
as 'I didn't mind'; 'I didn't think about it'; or,
'I didn't care'.

Pupils were also asked the reactions of their
friends to their being referred to a centre.
Almost half of the pupils thought that their
friends were indifferent toward their referral. A
third reported that their friends had made positive
remarks about the centre: 'they thought it would be

good for me'; and, 'those ones that had been here said they liked it'. However some of the 'positive' comments included remarks like: 'they said you don't do anything here'; and, 'they said it's a place to sit down and laze about in!'.

A fifth of the pupils mentioned friends' responses which might have reinforced their own negative reactions including: 'they thought it was a school for dunces'; 'they thought it was a mad school'; and, 'the ones that had been here didn't like it'. Surprisingly, however, only a few of the pupils whose friends had expressed negative comments about the centres, stated that they had, themselves, wholly negative reactions when they had been referred.

The mixture of feelings expressed to us illustrates the ambivalence that young people referred to centres feel about their position. We suspect that had interviews been carried out prior to placement, potential pupils may well have expressed more negative feelings. The comments they reported their friends had made may well have reflected their own feelings before they started at the centres. Having started there, however, most pupils then reported a positive view although, for some, the positive view was probably based on the idea of the centre being an easier option than ordinary school.

Spare-Time Interests
Pupils were asked to describe what they liked to do after school and at week-ends. The interests mentioned are shown in Table 4.3.

Table 4.3: Pupils' Interests

Type of activity	Percentage of pupils noting particular activity
Individual sports	30%
Pubs, discos, parties	29%
Playing out, 'hanging around' with friends	28%
Team sports	23%
Television	17%
Youth club	16%
Other indoor interests	14%
Cinema	12%
Working, Saturday job	11%
Indoor games	8%
Going out with boy/girlfriend	7%
Mechanics (cars and bikes)	5%
Other outdoor interests	4%

As Table 4.3 shows, pupils had a variety of interests. Some were characteristic of all youngsters - such as sports, going out with friends and watching television. Only one said he had no interests at all! A large number of comments referred to sports - both individual and team. Many pupils also reported 'hanging around with friends, playing out'; 'hanging round the flats'; 'going down the local shopping centre'; 'meeting friends in town'; and, 'playing out on bikes'.

Summary
The pupils who attended the centres were referred for two main reasons - disruption and non-attendance. The centres differed somewhat in the pupils they catered for: the majority of pupils at on-site and off-site support centres and educational guidance centres had been referred because of 'disruption'. The majority of those at voluntary agency centres and intermediate treatment schemes had been referred because of absenteeism or school refusal. Attendance was nevertheless said to be a problem for over two thirds of all the pupils.
The pupils ranged from 11 to 16 years; two thirds of the pupils, however, were in the 14 to 16 year old group. The proportions of pupils of different ages varied depending on the type of centre. In all except on-site centres, boys

outnumbered girls; in on-site centres girls outnumbered boys.

Nearly two thirds of the pupils were of English, Scottish, Welsh or Irish origin; a fifth had a Caribbean family background. More pupils in the centres than in ILEA as a whole, lived in single parent families or were 'in care'. The parents of pupils in centres were under-represented in the non-manual and skilled manual occupational categories but over-represented in the semi-skilled and unskilled categories. A greater proportion of pupils' parents were without a job than were the parents of ILEA secondary pupils as a whole.

As regards academic attainment, almost half of the pupils, at age 11, had been in the lowest Verbal Reasoning group, compared with only 25 per cent in the ILEA as a whole. Mathematics and reading tests revealed a large proportion of low scorers.

Over three-quarters of those interviewed said that they had stayed away from school on one or more occasions without a good reason. Seventy-five per cent of the pupils said that they had 'got into trouble' at school. The reasons most frequently mentioned included disruptive behaviour, poor relationships with teachers, violence towards other pupils, and opposition to rules. Half said that there were pupils in school with whom they did not get on and almost half said they used to get into fights, though the majority denied bullying or having been bullied.

The initial reactions to referral for over half of the pupils had been positive. Pupils' spare-time interests varied, but included sports and watching television as well as 'hanging around' with friends.

Chapter 5

STAFFING AT CENTRES

Introduction

In the previous chapter, we explored the characteristics of pupils who attend centres. In this chapter the focus is on those who work in them. The staff play a crucial role in determining whether or not the programme offered within centres will be a success or a failure for the pupils concerned. The relationships between teachers and pupils, and the morale of the staff are clearly amongst the factors which help determine how successful the centres will be.

The first section of the chapter presents information relating to the numbers of professional staff, their teaching assignments and other responsibilities. The second section is concerned with authority structures within centres, the relationships between staff, the relationships between staff and pupils, and the atmosphere in centres. The final section explores the effect of support centres on those who teach in them. It focuses on professional opportunities, in-service training and the dangers of professional isolation.

Professional Staff

A total of 97 professional staff were employed in the 32 centres (an average of 3 persons per centre). Of these, 82 were teachers and 15 were intermediate treatment or social workers. Of the teachers, 27 were part-time and the remaining 55 were mostly on scales 2 and 3 (24 and 17 respectively); nine were on scale 4 and five on scale 1.

There were, of course, considerable variations between types of centre both in the overall number of teachers involved and the number of teachers on different scale posts. Off-site support centres had, on average, 3.7 teachers on their staff, educational guidance centres 2.6 and voluntary agency centres and intermediate treatment schemes 2 teachers. On-site support centres had, on average, only 1.3 teachers per centre.

All of the education guidance centres, three off-site support centres and one intermediate treatment centre were headed by a scale 4 teacher. All other centres were headed by teachers on lower scales.

Sixty-four per cent of the staff were female and 36 per cent were male. Thirty-four per cent were under age 30, 43 per cent were between 30 and 40, 19 per cent were between 40 and 50 and 4 per cent were over age 50. Less than 7 per cent of the teachers had ethnic backgrounds outside the British Isles.

Of the teaching staff, a quarter possessed both a degree and a certificate of education, while a half had a certificate of education, but no degree. The remainder (25 per cent) had a degree, but no certificate of education. Almost half (46 per cent) of the teaching staff had taught for 5 years or less in mainstream or special education. Thirty-four per cent of the teachers had between 6 and 10 years teaching experience, 12 per cent had between 11 and 15 years and 8 per cent possessed 16 or more years of experience.

Teaching Assignments
Centre staff organised their teaching assignments in one of two ways. Either the teaching was divided equally amongst all staff, with each teacher preparing and teaching the full range of lessons, or assignments were divided on the basis of the teachers' training and experience. In one centre, for example, one teacher taught all mathematics and related subjects and a second teacher taught English and related subjects. So as to broaden the curriculum, eight centres also employed specialist teachers on a sessional basis, or recruited volunteers.

Teachers' other responsibilities
In addition to their teaching duties, many staff at the centres had further responsibilities:
Centre and programme administration, including organizing and preparing for committee meetings, preparing progress reports for case conferences, ordering supplies, arranging for guest teachers and

supply teachers, and, among voluntary agency centres, fund-raising and programme budgeting.
Clerical duties, concerned with attendance reports, book-keeping and writing to schools, the social services and other agencies.
Parent school and community liaison work including the maintenance of good working relationships with teachers, social workers, education welfare officers, medical officers and the pupils' families.
Other domestic duties including such tasks as meal preparation, cleaning and maintenance chores.

In addition to these tasks much time had to be allocated to talking with individual pupils. In some cases this involved chatting about pupils' interests or events in their lives, in others it involved counselling. Demands both for time and emotional support were made on the teachers and other adults who worked in the centres.

To enable centre staff to cope with these extra reponsibilities, 15 centres were closed to pupils for one half day per week. In addition, a number of the centres (six off-site support centres, three educational guidance centres and one intermediate treatment scheme) had clerical help for a period of between four and fifteen hours each week.

Despite this assistance, however, all but six of the directors or teachers-in-charge of centres reported that they had to work 'overtime' either during lunch-time, evenings or at weekends. The amount of 'overtime' was difficult for staff to quantify, but the majority estimated that they spent 4 to 10 hours each week of their own time on centre work and 19 per cent said the time they spent was more than 10 hours per week. It was felt by centre staff that there was a need for additional assistance in three main areas:

Professional staff. Many staff from all types of centres, except the on-site centres, commented on the desirability of using specialist teachers on a sessional basis. These centres would like to have had the flexibility to hire the necessary mathematics, science or foreign language teachers to broaden their curriculum.

Additional staff. Teachers in centres which did not have clerical assistance expressed the need for a part-time clerical officer. This, of course, did not apply to on-site centres, which had access to school secretaries. In addition a few of the staff in the voluntary agency centres felt the need for assistance with meal preparation and cleaning duties.

<u>Discretionary time.</u> Because of their small numbers, staff in all the centres, except on-sites, were unable to take breaks during the school day. All their time was spent with the pupils including the lunch hour, which created additional job-related stress. Moreover, it was sometimes very difficult for teaching staff to be released to attend professional training courses or conferences.

Authority structures of the centres

In order to provide some insight into the authority structures of the centres, we explored the way in which decisions were made. On the basis of interviews, observations and discussions with the staff, we have attempted to classify the centres into four types: the hierarchical, the democratic, the mixed hierarchical/democratic and the 'laissez-faire'.

In the hierarchical model the decision-making was solely the responsibility of those at the upper end of the hierarchy and there was little evidence of any discussion or consultation between staff at different levels. In the democratic model the decision-making was the responsibility of all, or most of, the staff and there appeared to be well-established procedures for making joint decisions. The mixed hierarchical/democratic model used a combination of different management styles. Thus, in some aspects of life in these centres the authority structure was clearly defined and important decisions taken only by senior staff; in other aspects, life was more democratic. In a few centres there was a 'laissez-faire' attitude to decision-making and each problem was dealt with in an idiosyncratic way. Inevitably, in these cases there appeared to be little consistency in centre management.

Of the 32 centres, the two largest groups were those which appeared to be organised on predominantly democratic principles (13 centres) and those run on the basis of mixed hierarchical/democratic principles (13 centres). The predominantly democratic group comprised more than half of each of the off-site support centres, the intermediate treatment schemes and the voluntary agency centres. The mixed hierarchical/democratic group, on the other hand, included half of the on-site centres and all of the educational guidance centres. Only one on-site centre could, in our judgment, most accurately be described as hierarchical in structure. Three centres appeared to function, at least for some of the time, in a laissez-faire fashion. Two of the centres were excluded from our attempts at classification as they were both staffed by only one teacher.

The formal structures of all centres are, of course, fundamentally hierarchical in nature. Titles, pay and levels of responsibility tend to be reflections of differences in the degrees of power of staff within centres. Thus for a centre to function according to the democratic model a deliberate decision had to be taken within the staff group to organise management in this way. The members of staff at the top of the formal hierarchy had to be willing to accede power to the other members of the staff for this form of structure to work.

Two of the factors which related to the way in which the centres were structured were the age and experience of the staff. In centres which veered towards the democratic model, the staff frequently were of similar age and had comparable levels of previous professional experience. In centres which were functioning according to mixed hierarchical/democratic principles the staff were often disparate either in age or in experience. Younger, less experienced staff reported that they were satisfied with the procedure whereby they were consulted but where the teacher-in-charge, or the director, made the final decisions.

Another factor related to the authority structure of the centres was the professional status of the staff. In the minority of centres, where staff were drawn from a variety of different disciplines, the tendency was for each professional group to insist on an equal voice in the decision-making procedures. A democratic form of structure also appeared to be more common in those centres where the various professions had responsibility for their own area of work and were sensitive about the status accorded to their specialism.

A further important factor which helped to determine the structure, especially in the intermediate treatment schemes and voluntary agency centres, was the basic philosophy on which they were founded. Many of the voluntary agency centres, for example, had been established by teachers who were fundamentally opposed to the hierarchical nature of secondary schools and who, as a result, set out to establish a different model of teaching and learning. One of the main tenets of such a philosophy was that all those involved in the activity should share in the decision-making process and should shoulder responsibility for the success or failure of the venture. Where staff held these views and where pupils were regarded as equal partners - at least in theory - the hierarchical model was clearly unacceptable.

It is, however, important to stress that, in addition to all these factors, the prevailing management style of the centres was affected by the personality of the people involved. Thus, for example, in a centre functioning on the basis of established democratic procedures, one member of staff was able, by force of personality, to impose his or her own preferences at times of group decision-making. Furthermore, where centres seemed to be functioning according to the laissez-faire model this did not appear to be intentional but was the result of a breakdown in the decision-making procedures.

In general, staff appeared to us to be most comfortable within a structure where it was obvious who had the ultimate responsibility and power. Within that basic framework however, where centres were organised on the basis of established democratic procedures and the staff genuinely participated in decision-making, there appeared to be a higher level of staff involvement in their work and in the commitment to its success. Thus those centres organised on the mixed hierarchical/democratic principles seemed to be those where staff had minimised the opportunities for unnecessary conflict and maximised the opportunities for genuine participation. Such an observation is, we realise, easy to make and we are conscious that such a management style can be extremely difficult to operate. The judgment of when to involve colleagues and when to take personal responsibility for a decision is seldom simple. It does appear, however, that this skill in judgment is one clear characteristic of leadership that the more successful directors of centres possessed.

Relationships between staff
In small units it is especially important that
relationships between staff are good. Pupils are
very quick to notice, and to exploit, inter-staff
tensions. This issue has been studied in a special
education setting. Laslett (1977), for example in
discussing the relationships between staff teaching
maladjusted children, notes that teachers'
attitudes to other personnel working in the
organisation directly affects their work. Disunity
among individuals concerned with the education of
maladjusted children disrupts what he calls the
'therapeutic endeavour' and weakens the
effectiveness of the institutions.

If this is true of special schools, it is even
more likely to be true of the small centres that we
were studying. Accordingly, we attempted to
investigate the amount of agreement that existed
amongst staff. So as to minimise any intrusion
into the personal lives of the staff we chose to
focus our investigation on the extent to which the
staff agreed about the aims and objectives of the
programme.

In our analysis of 30 centres (the same two
single-teacher centres are excluded) two large
groups (each of eight centres) were identified.
The first of these groups appeared to be best
described in terms of a consensus model. In this,
staff agreed about their aims and about the means
by which these should be achieved. In these
centres procedures had been established for
discussion of these topics and for resolving
conflicts or tensions. A higher proportion of the
off-site support centres and the intermediate
treatment schemes than of other types of centres
were found in this group.

The second group of centres included those
which appeared to have achieved a certain degree of
consensus, only for this to be broken by the
attitudes of one dominant member of the staff. A
smaller group of five centres appeared to function
with consensus on aims and objectives, but with
clear disagreement on the means by which such aims
should be achieved. In nine cases there did not
appear to be any consistent patterns at work,
generally because the centres were newly
established or had recently changed staff.

As might be expected, the extent to which the
staff agreed on aims and objectives and the ways
the differences were resolved appeared to be
closely related to the structure of the centres.

Where a good working structure has been established, it is obviously easier to obtain agreement on aims and objectives. Even if there are disagreements it is easier to resolve them. In contrast, where there is no clear structure the machinery to resolve disagreements - and the conflicts and tensions that can accompany them - is frequently missing.

In our view the importance of establishing a structure - of whatever type - is paramount. Staff will inevitably reflect the many different attitudes found in our society. Pupils, however, will find life in the centres much easier if there is reasonable agreement between staff. Hence the need for a mechanism whereby disagreements can be resolved. Such a view could, of course, be applied with as much relevance to a school (or to any other social institution) as to a centre. The difference in size of the two institutions, however, means that what is <u>advisable</u> for a school staff of forty teachers may be <u>essential</u> for a centre staff of four.

Relationships between staff and pupils

Laslett (1977), in discussing the relationships between staff and pupils at maladjusted schools, comments that teachers have the opportunity of helping the child to repair his or her relationships with adults. In his view teachers have the opportunity of helping the pupil to relate to other pupils by their management of the class. They also have the opportunity of assisting pupils acquire basic educational skills and of extending the child's knowledge and mastery of his or her environment. They can also provide the child with good models of social relationships. Such opportunities apply equally to staff of centres.

We decided to explore, therefore, the relationships between staff and pupils. We also hoped to judge the overall atmosphere prevailing in the centres. Although the atmosphere was influenced by the centre's organisation, its philosophy, and the characteristics of the staff and pupils, relationships between staff and pupils were also crucial.

Pupils were in centres primarily because of a breakdown in their relationships with their schools. Thus centre staff were faced with the difficult task of creating, or rebuilding, satisfactory relationships with pupils. In this, teachers used quite different approaches. Some concentrated solely on a teaching role using the low pupil-teacher ratio and the less formal atmosphere of a centre to provide individual teaching in basic skills. The rationale for this approach is that the pupils' lack of skills had probably been a prime factor in their being referred to a centre. By providing them with such skills, therefore, the teacher would be enabling pupils to cope with ordinary school. The same approach also included the teaching of social and survival skills as a preparation for a return to mainstream education.

A different role adopted by some teachers was that of a proxy-parent. In these cases, teachers would use their time with the pupil to discuss any personal or home difficulties. Methods varied from informal 'chats' to highly structured group or individual counselling sessions. Outings, holidays, visits to the pupil's home or even to the teacher's home, were all used as a means of promoting a relationship based on both care and control. In this way the teacher hoped to provide the pupil with the security and perhaps the affection that was believed essential to personal and social development.

Another role adopted by teachers was that of teacher-as-psychologist. This role did not seek to take the place of a parent, yet it gave priority to an interest in family relationships and to personal problems. In this role the teacher would use the time in the centre to explore the pupils' difficulties and attempt to explain these to the other people involved. In some cases the teacher would use his or her knowledge of, and interest in, counselling or some form of psychotherapy in order to work with pupils. Finally, there was the role of youth leader. In these cases there was less interest in academic tasks and more in social or sporting activities. Activities took place in evenings and holidays in addition to the ordinary time spent in centres.

These roles were not, in general, adopted and followed rigidly. Many centres would have teachers acting quite different roles; sometimes deliberately and sometimes according to the temperament of staff at centres. Such an arrangement could be extremely useful; to have one teacher lending an emphasis to the parental role, and another whose interests were in keeping with the youth leader role could balance the purely teaching roles of the other staff. Of course it was also possible for centres to place too great an emphasis on these other roles and to ignore the fundamental role of teacher. There is a temptation for other roles to appear more glamorous and, as a result, for teachers to undervalue their own skills. In our view this is a pity, for by doing so, they may neglect the simplest way of helping their pupils - by teaching them.

In general, the centres in our sample appeared to us to offer a balanced allocation of roles, and teaching was not neglected even when greater emphasis was placed on other roles. Eighteen of the centres (including most of the educational guidance centres and voluntary agency centres) appeared to emphasise a treatment role in which there was an emphasis on the alleviation of emotional or behavioural difficulties; seven centres stressed the acquisition of social skills and five centres concentrated primarily on the teaching of academic skills.

Survey of teaching staff - Professional opportunities

Of the 66 teachers (80 per cent of teachers in the centre sample) who participated in the survey, 32 were teachers-in-charge or directors and 34 were teaching staff. Those teachers not interviewed were mainly those teaching part-time at the centres.

Table 5.1 shows the number of teachers who had improved their status (by accepting a post within a centre) compared to those who had remained at the same scale and those who had accepted a lower post.

Table 5.1: Number of Teachers and their Professional Status

Professional status	On-site	Off-site supp	EGC	Vol. agcy	I.T.	Totals No.	%
Higher scale	4	14	8	4	7	37	56
No change	11	6	3	2	2	24	36
Lower scale	1	1	1	2	-	5	8
Total	16	21	12	8	9	66	100

For many of the teachers (56 per cent), accepting a post within a support centre had resulted in a promotion, while for others (36 per cent) it had been a transfer at the same level.

For a minority (8 per cent), the post was at a lower level than their previous one. Those teachers not promoted on entry reported other professional benefits, such as the pleasure of teaching an interesting group of pupils and the innovative and independent nature of the work.

HMI (1978), in their report on units for disruptive pupils, noted that many teachers in units were concerned about career prospects, working as they were, outside normal schools. It was with this in mind that we asked the centre teachers to describe their perceived opportunities for professional advancement.

On-site centre teachers did not feel that their careers were adversely affected by teaching in centres. All of the staff teaching in other types of centres, however, felt that career advancement might be a problem. This especially applied to teachers-in-charge. Most of these teachers considered that there was no more senior position into which they could move. They were also concerned that they would not be seen as suitable candidates for top level jobs within schools because of their absence from mainstream education.

When asked about their career plans, the teachers-in-charge gave a variety of responses. These can be seen in Table 5.2.

Table 5.2:   Career Plans of Teachers-in-Charge

Plans	Number of responses
Return to university for advanced degree	5
Deputy head of secondary school	3
Advisory staff	2
Year head within secondary school	2
Lateral move to another centre	7
Other, including clinical psychology	3
Total	22

The largest group indicated that the most likely move would be to another centre. Another sizeable group stated that a return to further study was their most likely next move. Others still, had ambitions to be deputy heads or to take on other posts.

The 28 other teachers in off-site support centres, educational guidance centres, voluntary agency centres, and intermediate treatment centres also perceived career advancement as a problem; however, they felt less affected than the teachers-in-charge. Eighteen (64 per cent) of these teachers hoped to advance to a higher post within their own or another support centre. Of the remaining ten teachers, three planned to return to university, three planned to pursue other professions such as counselling, and four hoped to return to mainstream education.

In-service training

In-service training is especially important to teachers in support centres because it affords opportunities for relevant teaching methods to be learned by those whose initial training seldom provided preparation for the tasks they now face. Such training also provides a forum for teachers to air their professional concerns. HMI (1978), however, found that the demands of close pupil-teacher contact made it difficult for individuals to be absent to attend courses or make visits to other centres.

In Table 5.3 teachers' perceptions of their opportunities for in-service training are given.

Table 5.3:   Teachers'   In-service   Training
Perceptions

	On-site	Off-site supp	EGC	Vol. agcy	I.T.	Totals No.	%
Adequate opportunities							
Yes	1	7	2	-	3	13	20
No	15	14	10	8	6	53	80
Time available:							
During school hours	1	5	2	-	5	13	20*
During evening hours	10	13	12	8	7	50	76*
Number who attended courses:							
Education course	7	3	4	2	2	18	27
Psychology course	5	2	8	2	3	20	30
Special education	2	1	3	-	1	7	11

* No information was available for 3 teachers.

Of the 66 teachers providing information, 13 (20 per cent) stated that opportunities for in-service training were adequate and 53 (80 per cent) stated that opportunities were not adequate. Many of these 53 teachers felt that there were no training courses available that directly related to support centre teaching. (In fact, several 'off-site' centre teachers were in the process of organising their own seminars.) Others stated that, given the staffing arrangements, it was not possible for one teacher to have leave for training.

Only 13 (20 per cent) teachers reported having in-service training opportunities during school hours. This was possible because some centres had more than two teachers (or had access to additional teachers) making it possible to release one person for short periods. Fifty (76 per cent) teachers

71

stated that they were able to attend in-service training during evening hours.

A total of 32 (49 per cent) teachers had attended one or more courses while at the centre. Most were enrolled on part-time university-based degree or diploma courses. Subjects studied included Education, Psychology and Special Education.

Professional isolation

Other research studies have commented on the 'professional isolation' experienced by those working in support centres. HMI (1978) noted that, despite the experience and qualifications of the large majority of teachers in units, working exclusively with disruptive pupils was a relatively new situation for most of them. In such a context most teachers were conscious of the pragmatic nature of much of their day-to-day work. Consequently, many felt uncertain, isolated and in need of the support and advice that would normally come through contact with others working with similar pupils.

Wilson & Evans (1980) also observed that, in autonomous units, there was a danger of isolation for the teachers. They found that those teachers working in attached units, received professional support from colleagues in the school, and concluded that teachers in ordinary schools with special classes were usually understanding and sympathetic towards the aims of their colleagues in the special classes. Similarly, Dawson (1980) noted that the teachers of classes attached to schools perceived much greater availability of help within the school than did those of the more autonomous units.

It was with these views in mind that we asked the teachers in the survey if they felt professionally isolated. These responses are shown in Table 5.4.

Table 5.4:   Professional Isolation

Isolation	On-site	Off-site supp	EGC	Vol. agcy	I.T.	Totals No.	%
Felt isolated	4	5	8	4	4	25	38
Did not feel isolated	10	12	4	4	3	33	50
Sometimes isolated/ sometimes not	2	4	-	-	2	8	12
Total	16	21	12	8	9	66	100

Half of the teachers said that they did <u>not</u> feel professionally isolated. However, 25 teachers (38 per cent) did suffer feelings of professional isolation and eight teachers (12 per cent) felt this for some of the time. More of the EGC staff (8 out of 12) felt professionally isolated than teachers in other types of centres.

The most frequent reasons given by teachers for not feeling isolated were: that the centre was part of a school (30 per cent of those who did not feel isolated); that they had frequent and varied contacts with schools and outside agencies (27 per cent); that they attended training courses (24 per cent) and that they received support from other centre staff (24 per cent).

The reasons given by teachers for feeling isolated in the centres included: 'an ill-defined role and no professional colleagues' (64 per cent); the lack of stimulation from a large school setting 'including break-time discussions with staff' (40 per cent) and 'no professional tradition or forum for discussions' (24 per cent).

As an indication of job satisfaction, we also asked teachers the length of time they planned to remain in their current posts. Their responses are shown in Table 5.5.

Table 5.5: Length of Time Centre Teachers Plan to Remain in Posts

Length of time	On-site	Off-site supp	EGC	Vol. agcy	I.T.	Totals No.	%
Less than 1 year	5	7	5	1	5	23	35
2-3 years	7	7	5	5	1	25	38
4 or more years	4	7	2	2	3	18	27
Total	16	21	12	8	9	66	100

Thirty-five per cent of the teachers planned to leave within less than one year. Thirty-eight per cent planned to stay for 2 to 3 years and 27 per cent for four years or longer. Interestingly, however, only a few cited job dissatisfaction as the primary reason for wishing to leave.

Summary
This chapter has attempted to describe the teachers working in the support centres in our sample. We are conscious, however, that by providing information on age or experience or by describing the particular roles we observed in the centres, we are giving only a very limited picture of the teachers. In order, therefore, to complement this information we should say that our general impression was of a dedicated group of staff dealing with pupils acknowledged to be difficult. These staff worked in far from ideal conditions, often felt isolated, and used skills in which they had had no formal training. Furthermore, unlike teachers in ordinary schools, they did not have breaks and lunch hours in which they could relax away from their pupils. Despite this, teachers appeared willing to give up their own time to engage in activities with pupils.
Many of these teachers obviously found the setting of the centres more congenial than that of an ordinary school. The lack of formality, the focus on the individual development of pupils, and the freedom from the examination-dominated curriculum of secondary schools clearly appealed to them. Nevertheless, as we have noted, a number of teachers were concerned that future career advancement might be limited. Having accepted a

74

promotion to a post in a centre, some teachers were now worried that it would be increasingly difficult to get out.

Whilst the sixties and early seventies had seen a proliferation of pastoral posts in schools - for which experience in a centre would provide a valuable qualification - one of the effects of falling rolls has been to slow down promotion and to limit the opportunities available to teachers. For those on lower scales in the centres there still existed the possibility of promotion either in the same centre or in another, but for those on the higher scales the outlook was less hopeful.

Despite this concern over career development, the morale of the staff we interviewed was generally high. They were doing a difficult job without having as much support as they would have liked, but nevertheless they believed it to be important and worthwhile. We could not, however, ignore the anxiety expressed over long-term plans. If, owing to patterns of movement in the teaching force, centre staff find themselves trapped in a career blind alley, the consequences for morale and for the effective running of the centres may well be serious.

Chapter 6

HOW CENTRES WORK

Introduction
In the two previous chapters we discussed the
characteristics of the pupils who attend centres
and the teaching staff who work in them. In this
chapter, we shall be concerned with the centres and
how they function. Other studies of support
centres have looked at certain aspects of centre
life - such as the curriculum and the referral
procedures. In addition to exploring these
aspects, we have attempted to obtain a fuller
picture of centre life and of how centres work.
The areas covered include academic assessment,
teaching styles and the reintegration of pupils
into school. To complement this factual approach,
pupils' views on centre life were also sought.
    This chapter is divided into three main
sections. The first section focuses on the details
of how centres are administered. The second
section deals with what actually goes on in centres
- how pupils are referred, their academic
assessment, the curriculum and the teaching styles
adopted. The type of rules and regulations,
controls and sanctions, and the pupils' views of
these and on centre life generally are presented.
In addition, the links between centres and schools,
community agencies and pupils' families are
discussed. The third section is concerned with the
centres and how pupils are prepared for school
reintegration. Finally, there is a discussion of
pupils' perceptions of their own future.

Administrative Arrangements

1. Management Committees
All the 'off-site' centres had been established
with some form of management committee. These

generally included representatives from divisional office and from any schools served, together with education welfare officers and the teacher-in-charge of the centre. The committees of educational guidance centres included psychologists, and those of intermediate treatment schemes also had representatives from the local social services. The committees of voluntary agency centres usually included parents and representatives from the community.

The functions of the management committees varied from centre to centre. In some cases they were closely involved in all aspects of the programme whereas, in others, they were concerned primarily with the overall planning and policy decisions, with the problems of individual pupils, with links between schools, or with the reintegration of pupils to mainstream schooling.

2. Management by an individual

Almost all of the on-site centres were administered by the school's headteacher, the deputy head or the teacher-in-charge of pastoral care. The functions performed by these individuals varied considerably. Some senior staff were involved only in the overall planning and policy decisions relating to the centres, whereas others were also concerned with decisions on pupil intake and the day-to-day running of the programme.

The staff at on-site and off-site support centres and at educational guidance centres were generally satisfied with the management arrangements. However, staff from several centres expressed their dissatisfaction with what they perceived to be the committee's inability to provide adequate professional support. Teachers blamed this on the tendency of committees to view programmes in abstract terms removed from the day-to-day activities of centres.

Many staff from voluntary agency centres and intermediate treatment schemes were dissatisfied with current arrangements. They thought committee members were too diverse in their professional interests and were not sufficiently involved with the operation of the programme. In many centres teachers felt management support was fragmented. However, on the positive side, representatives on committees, with their varied backgrounds, had often proved to be a good source of contacts in the community.

3. Decision-making

In order to ascertain how the key management decisions were made, centre staff were asked a range of questions about divisions of responsibility.

In general, we found that responsibility for major programme decisions appeared to rest with appropriate bodies. ILEA administrators and management committees were responsible for policy areas, such as the structure of the programme, the size of the centre and the choice of staff. Staff in the centres were responsible for decisions regarding the curriculum, extra-curricular activities and the choice of educational materials. However, approximately one third of the centres looked to the parent schools for decisions regarding the curriculum and for advice on the return of pupils to school.

The most controversial decision area concerned admissions, namely, who decided which pupils were admitted to the centres. As the support centres were designed to serve schools, school heads and management committees felt that they should have the final say on admissions. Centre staff, however, felt that whether their programmes would succeed or fail depended largely on the pupils admitted. Since centre programmes were designed for pupils of different ages with different behavioural problems, staff members thought that admission decisions should be within their control as they felt they were best placed to make these decisions.

We found that just over half of the centres made their own admission decisions, either through the director or by involving all centre staff. In the remaining centres, admissions were the responsibility of the management committees.

Although generally satisfied with these decision-making arrangements, staff in many centres felt that the large number of people and committees involved resulted in fragmented management and, on occasion, gave rise to problems. Many centre staff, for example, felt that they should have more say in choosing new staff, since centre teachers (normally only two or three in number) worked very closely together. Others felt that the teacher-in-charge should have more authority. In contrast, some staff expressed the view that parent schools should be more directly involved in programme decisions, especially when deciding on a pupil's return to school.

Functioning of Centres

1. Referral Procedures

HMI (1978) in their study of units discuss referral procedures. Their findings will be outlined before our own are presented.

HMI found that the various procedures which had been developed for the referral of pupils reflected different philosophies and objectives. The most marked differences were between off-site units serving a number of schools and on-site units serving one school. For on-site units it was rare to find reference to agencies outside the school. Admission was channelled formally through a committee of senior staff; in such cases, the teacher-in-charge worked closely with appropriate members of staff. As off-site units nearly always served a number of schools, with a consequent limit on places, careful appraisal of entrants was undertaken. The initiative for admission to a unit could come from a number of different sources; in schools it was usually channelled through the headteacher, but education welfare officers were as likely to report truants and school phobics as were social service workers and probation officers. HMI also noted that children had been known to refer themselves and anxious parents had personally approached some teachers in charge of units. The part played by educational psychologists ranged from giving professional advice on specific referrals through membership of admissions panels, to having the final word on all referrals.

In our study, referral procedures varied from centre to centre. However, in most off-site support centres, voluntary agency centres and intermediate treatment schemes, a rather similar procedure emerged. In these centres, the referral was initiated by the pupil's parent school, education welfare officer, or some other agency (e.g., social services). The centre staff then reviewed the referral and obtained background information on the pupil. This was collected in a variety of ways: some collected copies of school and medical records, some asked teachers to complete their own forms, and others relied on information collected less formally - by telephone for example. Some centres then held a case conference to discuss the pupil. However in other centres, staff felt that such conferences were time-consuming and not very fruitful. Approximately one third of the centres made use of a trial period before enrolling the child on a long-term basis.

Referral procedures for on-site centres were the least formal. Generally, a head or deputy discussed a pupil who was in need of extra support with the centre's teacher-in-charge. These staff decided the best course for the child, worked out a timetable for the pupil's attendance at the centre, and the pupil followed this course.

Educational psychologists were officially responsible for initiating referrals to educational guidance centres. A standardised referral form was completed by the headteacher and the school's educational psychologist who then interviewed the child and the parents. The educational psychologist then contacted the director of the centre who, in turn, met with the child, and an admission decision was made. All of the educational guidance centres followed this procedure. However, frequency of contacts with the educational psychologist and the formality of written reports, varied.

The length of time taken to process referrals ranged from less than one week (all on-site centres) to 36 weeks. However, most referrals were processed within 8 weeks. All centres cited 'available space' as the primary cause of delays. For those centres with available space, 'meeting with parents' and 'awaiting school records' were both given as reasons for delays in the process.

Most of the centre staff felt that their referral processes were relatively efficient and effective. However, three suggestions for improvement were made:

1) Closer communication with referring schools and agencies should be encouraged by directors, so that the number of inappropriate referrals could be minimised.

2) Head teachers should ensure that their staff understand the necessity of providing background information to support referrals.

3) Centre staff should have a 'veto power' over admission decisions in those centres where these were taken by outside management.

The first and second suggestions concern the need for closer co-operation between schools and centres. The third suggestion illustrates the desire of teachers working in centres to control admissions. It brings into the open a fundamental conflict between the needs of centre staff and the needs of head teachers of local schools. We will discuss this conflict in our final chapter.

Academic assessment

Laslett (1977) sees a well planned assessment programme as important since it enables teachers to become aware of children's needs as soon as possible. This makes it easier to plan appropriate remedial work and helps children to understand the relevance of lessons and activities included in the curriculum. Dawson (1980) looked at units' assessment and recording of pupils' progress. He found that around half of all units used standard IQ and attainment tests during the selection of pupils and during a pupil's attendance at a centre.

We found that the collection of information about pupils' educational background was part of most centres' referral procedure. However, in many cases this information was provided inconsistently or was not specific enough to enable a pupil's curriculum to be planned. Many centres, therefore, carried out their own testing and assessment.

Most on-site centres relied on the assessment procedures of the parent school but some made their own informal assessments of basic abilities and of motivation. Of the other centres, half carried out formal tests of reading and mathematics at the time of admission and just under half assessed pupils' abilities on the basis of work done during the first few weeks. Only one centre reported that no assessments were made of pupils skills and abilities.

Almost all the centres used academic assessment as a basis for planning the curriculum and lessons. Over a third of the staff in these centres - particularly those in voluntary agency centres and intermediate treatment schemes - did not administer formal tests. This was for two reasons: their belief that test results were unreliable; and because it was felt that test taking was, for many pupils, a traumatic experience.

Curriculum

Other studies have explored the curriculum of units. HMI (1978) in their survey found that the range of subjects taught in the units was variable.

81

While English and mathematics were taught in almost every unit, other academic subjects such as history, geography and science appeared far less frequently. Modern languages, religious education and music were taught in only a very small minority of centres. This pattern meant that for many pupils in units the range of school subjects available was limited. HMI also found that some units lacked specialist resources, particularly text-books, other reference materials and works of fiction. Dawson (1980) found a 'core curriculum' at most units comprising English language, mathematics, art and craft and physical education and allied subjects, supported by one or more of the humanities.

In our own study of the curriculum, we were concerned about the comparability of centre and 'parent school' education. We surveyed the curricula followed in centres - including the basis for selecting courses - and the degree to which the centres followed a similar curriculum to the schools.

The curriculum at all on-site centres was designed to duplicate the pupil's normal class work. Since most pupils attended these centres part-time, and on a lesson-by-lesson basis, this consisted of work set by a class teacher and supervised by the centre teacher. It also included work designed to provide additional instruction for difficult subject areas, some remedial education and counselling sessions to address pupils' problems of social and emotional adjustment.

The subjects taught in 'off-site' centres are shown in Table 6.1.

Table 6.1:   Number of 'Off-Site'   Centres Offering
Various Subjects

Subjects	Off-site support N=8	E.G.C. N=5	Vol. agcy. centre N=4	IT scheme N=5	All centres N=22
English	8	5	4	5	100%
Mathematics	8	5	4	5	100%
Biology	4	2	3	4	59%
Chemistry	1	0	0	1	9%
Science	3	0	2	3	36%
History	8	5	4	5	100%
Foreign Languages	2	0	1	2	23%
Drama,Music	1	1	3	2	32%
Art and Craft	8	5	4	4	95%
Games	8	4	4	5	95%
Other	1	3	1	2	32%

Most off-site support centres tried to
duplicate the parent school's curriculum. All
offered English, mathematics, history, art and
craft and games. Many centres, however, were
hampered by lack of specialist teachers and
equipment, particularly as far as foreign language
and science teaching were concerned. Those centres
that were able to offer these subjects did so
either because, by chance, the staff were trained
to teach these subjects, or because the staff went
to considerable lengths to prepare themselves to
teach subjects other than their own specialisms.
    All of the educational guidance centres
attempted to duplicate the parent school
curriculum. Most centres provided instruction
using parent school materials. However these
centres, like the off-site support centres, had too
few teaching resources.
    Most of the voluntary agency centres and
intermediate treatment schemes duplicated the
mainstream curriculum only for specific subjects,
(e.g., English, mathematics, history) or when a
pupil selected an examination option. Otherwise,
they developed their curriculum plans
independently. Since most of the pupils on these
schemes were 'older' secondary pupils and had been
out of school for long periods and were not likely
to return to school, more emphasis was placed on

providing basic instruction and work-oriented training.

Teaching Styles

Few studies have explored the teaching styles adopted by centre staff. One exception was Dawson (1980), who found that units using team-teaching were rare. When asked to say in what ways their methods differed from those of pupils' parent schools, over 90 per cent of respondents stated that their units had a greater degree of individualised teaching than had the parent schools.

We looked in some detail at teaching styles and found a variety of practice, including teacher-directed group work, team teaching, individual pupil work programmes, and pupil-based group work. In the first two of these, the teacher was likely to be the central figure with the pupil in the role of recipient. In the last two, the pupil was likely to have a more prominent role in instigating and carrying out the work.

Each style of teaching was more suited to some situations than others. The styles which appeared to be most prevalent in each centre, tended to be related to various pupil, staff and organisational characteristics. The number of pupils in the centre, their age range and abilities all appeared to influence the teaching style adopted. The more similar the pupils were in their personal characteristics, the more likely it was that they would be taught in groups rather than on an individual basis. Thus, for example, in on-site centres, where pupils were more likely to be of differing ages and ability, individual pupil work programmes were widely used.

Another factor which appeared to affect the extent to which each style was used in the centre, was the centre's relationship to the school system. On-site centres, for example, were more closely related to their parent schools. Pupils were thus more likely to come to the centre equipped with their own individual work programme – often in the subject areas being covered by the class from which they were withdrawn. This was least likely to occur in voluntary agency centres and intermediate treatment schemes. In these centres, pupils were more likely to be allowed to participate in the planning of their own work. Where centres were providing all or most of the pupils education (i.e., the majority of the 'off-site' centres) they were more likely to use a range of different techniques in their overall teaching plan in an attempt to provide for all or most of the pupils' educational needs.

We classified the centres according to the style which appeared to be most prevalent in each centre. By this criterion, the largest group of centres (half of the total number) were those where an individual pupil work programme was the model most widely used for learning. This method was used in a high proportion of on-site centres and intermediate treatment schemes. Most of the centres combined this approach with teacher-directed work or team teaching.

In the second largest group of centres (a third of the sample), teacher-based group work appeared to be the predominant style. This group comprised a high proportion of off-site support centres and educational guidance centres. Again, both individual pupil work and team-teaching models and to a lesser extent, pupil-based group work were used. Only one educational guidance centre appeared to make the most use of the team-teaching approach, again in conjunction with the teacher-directed group method plus an individual work programme for pupils.

Lastly, three centres (one intermediate treatment scheme and two voluntary agency centres) gave priority to the pupil-based small group work approach, but also used the teacher lecturing style and individual pupil work programmes.

Activities used to support teaching

Earlier studies have noted that support centres frequently supplement their ordinary curriculum with specialised teaching techniques (e.g., HMI, 1978). Most of the support centres in our study also made use of specialised teaching techniques. These included remedial education and special classes as well as the use of guest instructors, field trips, role modelling and group dynamics.

Remedial Education

We found that many of the pupils admitted to support centres needed basic education and all but two of the 32 centres provided it. Two-thirds of the centres had at least one staff member who had specialised training or experience teaching remedial classes. These findings are in line with those of other researchers such as HMI (1978).

Special classes and guest instructors

All centres in our sample supplemented normal academic work with specialised classes designed to teach a range of skills. Examples included, photography, film making, interior decorating and producing a local newspaper. In addition, pupils in several centres were responsible for preparing lunch or assisting with the centre's clerical duties. Many centres invited representatives from various community agencies to talk to centre pupils about their work and what it involved. Amongst those invited were police officers and careers counselling officers. Likewise HMI (1978) found that visiting staff were deployed to teach a range of practical and vocational subjects including motor mechanics, catering and guitar playing, and to provide careers education.

Field trips

HMI (1978) also noted that teachers in units frequently provided a varied range of other activities in order to complement the limited number of academic subjects offered. These included squash, skating, fell-walking, sea-fishing, residential holidays, camping, youth hostelling, and visits to places of interest. In our study, we found that most off-site centres arranged regular outings for the pupils to museums, shopping centres, recreational centres and sporting events. These trips contained elements of the 'hidden curriculum' - as one teacher said: 'For some youngsters, sitting in a mini-bus for a half hour or going horse riding can be a major achievement towards gaining social or 'survival-type' skills'.

Role modelling

Teachers consciously set themselves up as 'models' as the primary means of teaching dress style and such social skills as table manners and daily etiquette. They also presented constructive ways to express such feelings as anger and frustration.

Group dynamics

Many centres structured part of their programme on the basis of group dynamics, whereby staff and pupils all participated in regularly scheduled discussion and where, in theory, all had an equal say. These group sessions were most frequently used for deciding about extra activities and were seen as teaching problem-solving, decision-making and other 'survival' skills.

In addition to these activities, the teachers at all the centres stressed the importance to the success of the programme of a warm caring approach by the staff. To us, as observers, it certainly appeared that such an approach was important but obviously needs to be part of a carefully thought out structure for the programme.

What the pupils thought about the centres

Very little work has been undertaken to discover pupils' views on centres although Wilson & Evans (1980) note that 'when it was possible to determine the pupils' attitudes these were usually favourable to the special unit and sometimes very critical of the referring school'.

We asked pupils to comment on the differences between parent schools and centres. We also asked what they liked or disliked about the centres. Finally we asked what benefits they thought they had gained from attending the centres.

Differences from school

The most frequently occurring comments reflected a congenial atmosphere at the centre and satisfactory relationships with centre staff. Nearly a quarter of the pupils, for instance, described relationships with centre teachers as good; their comments included: 'the teachers are more friendly', 'you get treated like adults' and 'you can talk over problems with teachers'.

The fact that they were better able to study at the centre was mentioned by a fifth of those interviewed, they made such comments as: 'able to do more work than at school' and 'better able to concentrate'.

Positive comments about the general atmosphere were made by 18 per cent of the pupils and included: 'you have your say in things' and 'it's like someone's home here'. These pupils obviously felt a general warmth and friendship in the centres.

Sixteen per cent of the pupils enjoyed life at the centres for rather different reasons. They remarked that life at the centre involved 'less work' and made such comments as 'you don't work to a complete timetable' and 'you only do lessons in the morning'. Others (16 per cent) commented on the break-time activities, which reflected the more relaxed atmosphere of some centres such as 'being allowed to smoke', 'drinking tea' and 'sitting inside during break'. Some pupils (15 per cent) enjoyed outside activities such as 'free outings' and 'going to the pictures'.

Twelve per cent of pupils commented positively about other pupils in the centre, making such remarks as: 'it's a smaller group here' and 'children are more friendly'.

The comments about the curriculum followed in centres and school, included remarks by over a fifth of the pupils that the subjects studied at the centre were different from those at school or that working patterns were different generally. Others (12 per cent) commented more specifically on the freedom of choice in the subject studied. Comments included 'you choose your own timetable' and 'do things because you want to do them'. This reflected the policy in some centres of involving the pupils in the planning of their own work programme, a feature which is generally less possible in schools. Some pupils (9 per cent) mentioned doing 'better subjects' at the centres, commenting that 'you do subjects relevant to the job you want' and 'subjects are more interesting'. A few pupils (8 per cent) remarked on the 'shorter work periods' at the centre, whilst others (7 per cent) commented on the 'longer work periods'.

It was apparent from their answers to all the questions that the pupils liked being at the centres. Only 4 per cent made comments indicating that they disliked the centre, whilst a further 8 per cent of the pupils were non-committal.

Pupils were asked about which particular features of centre life they enjoyed. Their responses are shown in Table 6.2.

Table 6.2:   The Good Things About Centres

Features	Percentage of pupils noting feature N=162
English and maths - basic skills	48%
Creative arts and crafts	27%
Other activities in centre	26%
Good centre atmosphere	22%
Outings	19%
Academic - other than basic skills	12%
Relationships between teachers and pupils	9%
Break-time activities	9%
Everything	7%

The most frequent positive response was 'English and mathematics' - basic skills - mentioned by half the pupils. A number of others (12 per cent) also enjoyed other academic subjects. These included science, computer studies, social studies and special projects. It would appear that many centre pupils enjoyed their academic studies in a setting different from their original school. Art and craft, and outings were also clearly important for many pupils.

Some pupils also commented on the favourable atmosphere and the good relationships between teachers and pupils at the centre. For a number, the good thing about their education was 'other pupils in the centre' or 'the environment of the centre' or 'making the tea' or 'cooking the lunch'. In one centre some pupils said that they liked coming in on Friday when the centre was officially closed, but when voluntary attendance was welcome.

Comments about the relationship between teachers and pupils included: 'like the way we are taught', 'attention', 'helpful teachers' and 'the way the centre is run'.

Pupils were also asked to say what they disliked about the centres.

Table 6.3: The Bad Things About Centres

Features	Percentage of pupils noting feature N=162
Nothing	59%
Rules	11%
Other centre pupils	9%
Facilities/location	9%
Centre teachers	7%
Too few academic subjects	6%
Everything	7%

Most pupils said that there was nothing they disliked. Others disliked some aspects of centre life - for example, the rules such as 'no talking in lessons' and 'doing the washing up'. Some disliked aspects of the location, such as the distance from home and others disliked the facilities or dinner. Others mentioned disliking other pupils at the centre, complaining about 'bad behaviour', 'other kids scrounging fags' or 'no other pupils of the same sex'.

Benefits from Centres

In order to gauge their feelings about the value of their time at the centre we asked 'What do you think you get out of the centre?' Their responses are shown in Table 6.4.

Table 6.4: The Benefits of Centres

Benefits	Percentage of pupils noting benefit N=162
Academic progress	51%
Learning to cope with, and solve, own problems	25%
Reintegration into school	18%
Positive relationship with staff	11%
Everything	11%
Social skills, discussion skills	9%
Preparation for work and adult life	9%

Over half the pupils mentioned academic benefits, such as: 'you learn more', 'better education', 'got more help with work', 'catch up on reading and spelling' and 'learn to do the work properly'.

A quarter of the pupils referred to the help they felt they were receiving in solving their problems. Comments included: 'learning not to talk too much', 'learning not to lose your temper', 'makes you more grown up', 'you avoid trouble in class', 'better concentration'. Some made remarks about avoiding being taken to court for non-attendance at school.

Another benefit concerned future reintegration into school and included comments such as 'gets you settled into school' indicating that, for these pupils at least, returning to school was likely to be the main benefit of their centre experience.

The series of comments referring to 'positive relationships with staff' included comments like: 'can ask teachers about work' and 'teachers are more human'.

Comments referring to 'social skills and group discussion' included: 'gives you self-confidence', 'mix with people better', 'smaller group' and 'helped me find out what I'm really like'.

The category 'preparation for work and adult life' included: 'to get a job that I want to do' and 'a good report for starting work'.

Only 7 per cent of the pupils said that they had gained nothing from their experience at the centre.

The positive feelings that the children generally held about attending the centres, were reflected in their attitudes to being absent from the centres. When asked how often they stayed away from the centre without a reason, most pupils (60 per cent) said that they had never been absent. However, almost a third said they had been absent. Most of these had stayed away occasionally, although some had stayed away regularly for periods of up to two weeks and an even smaller number (four pupils) said that they had been absent for long stretches of over two weeks.

Range and type of rules and regulations

The standard of pupils' behaviour was a major concern in the centres as the entire teaching programme was dependent on the pupils behaving in an acceptable and appropriate manner.

Over half of the centres appeared to have fairly extensive rules. These were usually very similar to those which exist in mainstream schools and concerned time-keeping, the wearing of school uniform, refraining from eating, smoking, and talking during lessons and so on. The remaining centres had a considerably shorter list of established rules, but these often included all-embracing requirements such as finishing a set piece of work every morning, or 'behaving in a way acceptable to the staff'.

The consistency with which the rules were applied varied from centre to centre, depending partly on the structure and philosophy of the centre but more frequently on the personalities of the staff involved. The centres could be classified into two groups according to whether rules were enforced <u>consistently</u>, or whether there was a degree of <u>flexibility</u> in their application. Just under half of the centres were consistent in the way they enforced their rules and a similar proportion were flexible. The four remaining centres were considered to be 'very flexible'.

The judgment of when or when not to insist on strict application of rules, is, of course, extremely difficult to make. Very flexible rules can mean that in reality nobody takes any notice of them. In the same way an over strong emphasis on consistency can lead to difficulties with a particularly disturbed pupil. Highly skilled teachers seemed to have learned how and when to be flexible.

Control techniques and sanctions

We decided to explore the range and prevalence of specific techniques and strategies used by staff to control behaviour and maintain an orderly working environment in the centres.

Differences between centres were apparent, as in some centres the control of pupil behaviour was considered to be solely the concern of the staff, while in others the pupil group as a whole was seen as a useful means of controlling wayward pupils. The practice of a staff member dealing individually with a pupil who was misbehaving appeared to be universal; however, nearly half of the centres (particularly educational guidance centres and voluntary agency centres) also appeared to try and involve the other pupils in censuring unacceptable behaviour in their peers. In fact, a third of the centres actually arranged group sessions with staff and pupils. In these sessions rules and behaviour were discussed and group decisions regarding rewards and sanctions for particular behaviours were taken.

In addition three specific strategies were used to control behaviour: direct confrontation together with sanctions; anticipation of imminent trouble; and some form of behaviour modification techniques.

In half of the centres staff appeared to favour confronting directly the recalcitrant pupil with his or her unacceptable behaviour and dealing with it by means of relevant sanctions. These sanctions included the withdrawal of privileges (such as a promised outing), discussion with his or her parents or, if the incident was of sufficient seriousness, temporary exclusion from the centre. The use of direct confrontation and sanctions occurred in all types of centres, but was particularly prevalent in on-site centres and educational guidance centres.

Another management technique which appeared to be a very effective tool for controlling behaviour was 'anticipation'. This technique required the staff to maintain a fairly tight control of the activities of the group; they they also had to be alert for any disorder or conflict. Potentially disturbing incidents were thus anticipated and attempts made to defuse the situation. This technique appeared to be more prevalent in some centres than others and seemed to be related to the presence of teachers who had developed the ability to control pupils in this way. Behaviour modification techniques based on the giving of rewards did not appear to be widely used except in educational guidance centres.

In sum, the centres appeared to be using a whole range of different techniques and strategies for controlling the behaviour of pupils in their charge.

Pupils' views of rules and sanctions

In order to ascertain the pupils' own perceptions of the rules at the centre, they were simply asked: 'What are the rules here?' The pupils' responses are shown in Table 6.5

Table 6.5:   Rules at the Centre - Pupils' Views

Rules	% of pupils noting each rule (N=162)
Rules about smoking	31%
Rules 'like school rules'	28%
Rules about behaviour at centre	22%
Rules about behaviour in class	15%
Rules about organisation/ convenience	15%
Rules about behaviour with peers	14%
Rules about work	10%
Rules about punctuality	9%
Rules about attendance	6%
No rules	6%
Rules 'different from school rules'	3%

The table shows that the rule remembered by most pupils (31 per cent) related to smoking – perhaps because this was an activity which most often brought pupils into conflict with the staff. A proportion of pupils (28 per cent) saw little difference between school rules and those of the centre. However, nearly half of those pupils were in on-site centres and so would still be aware of the general influence of school.

The category 'behaviour in class' (15 per cent) included comments on behaviour during lessons whilst 'behaviour at the centre' (22 per cent) included comments about appropriate behaviour during breaks and lunch. The category 'organisation/convenience' covered those rules considered necessary for the efficient running of the centre, including washing-up one's own plate after lunch and other 'chores'. Comments in the 'work' category included such rules as 'no lazing about' or 'not being allowed to play football until you've done your work'.

In on-site centres the most frequently occurring comments (40 per cent) referred to centre rules being like those in the rest of the school. In off-site support centres and educational guidance centres, 27 per cent of the pupils' comments referred to rules on smoking, possibly because this regulation was seen as one of the established rules. In voluntary agency centres, 26 per cent of pupils' comments concerned 'organisation/convenience' rules. In intermediate treatment schemes, the most frequently occurring comment referred to 'behaviour in the centre in general' (20 per cent). Fifteen per cent of the comments referred to 'behaviour in class', while the emphasis on smoking was slightly less marked (13 per cent). It is interesting to note that the pupils in both voluntary agency centres and intermediate treatment schemes made no comparison between the centre and school - this may reflect the very different environment in these types of centres, from that in the ordinary school.

Pupils were also asked what happened when they broke rules or misbehaved. A summary of their most frequent responses is shown in Table 6.6.

Table 6.6: Pupils' Perceptions of Sanctions

Sanctions	% of pupils noting sanction N = 162
Verbal expression of disapproval by staff	46%
Exclusion	38%
Parental involvement	14%
Withdrawal of privileges	9%
Group discussion	6%
Nothing	6%

The most frequently occurring comments referred to the 'verbal expression of disapproval' by centre staff. This category contained a variety of comments on teachers' responses to misbehaviour, including being 'talked to', being 'told off' and the staff 'having a go at you!'

The second largest group of comments in all types of centre referred to 'exclusion'. This category contained comments referring to withdrawal from the centre and ranged from being sent to the senior staff in the school (on-site centres only), to being sent home to 'cool off' or expulsion. 'Parental involvement', ranking third in frequency, referred to the centre teachers enlisting parental support in the event of a pupil's misbehaviour.

Overall, then, the large number of comments referring to 'verbal expression of disapproval', shows that teachers in centres, like those in schools, mainly rely on telling pupils off. Unlike school, however, no pupils reported being made to write lines or being given detentions.

Links with schools, community agencies and pupils' families

Support centres, when established, were intended to provide schools with a special resource and, as such, form part of the total education system. However, these centres - and especially the 'off-site' ones - are separate units depending for the smooth operation of their programmes upon the maintenance of good relationships with 'parent' schools, other community agencies and pupils' families.

Since parent schools were involved in referring pupils and, in some cases, with the curriculum followed at the centre, we studied the type and frequency of centres' contacts with parent schools.(1) The number of schools served by support centres ranged from one school to all secondary schools in the ILEA division. On average the centres served six to eight schools.

Half of the teachers in charge of off-site support centres reported frequent and satisfactory contact with parent schools; the remaining ones reported good relationships with some of parent schools and less satisfactory relationships with others. The less co-operative schools were characterized as being uninterested, withholding referral information, and being unavailable to centre staff. The staff at off-site support centres considered that several factors contributed to poor relationships with schools. These included the location of the centre, misunderstandings about the centre's objectives, inappropriate referrals, and a general shortage of school and centre staff-time.

All of the educational guidance centres were designed as a division-wide resource. Pupils attending them came from up to 15 secondary schools in any one division. All the staff reported good relationships with their parent schools. Contacts were frequent and there was a regular exchange of written and verbal information about pupils' progress. However, many staff felt that they needed to increase contact with classroom teachers over the planning of the centre curriculum and the part-time return of pupils to school.

Staff in voluntary agency centres and intermediate treatment schemes were less concerned

---

(1) On-site centres, because they are part of their 'parent' school, are not included here.

with parent school relationships because their pupils had been out of school for long periods and frequently were not known to school staff. Staff from several of these centres, however, hoped to improve relations with parent schools as far as guidance on curriculum content (for example, for 'O' level and CSE examinations) was concerned.

There were two types of community agencies with which centres had frequent contact. One was the 'helping' agencies such as the social and family services, medical services, job counselling and placement agencies and institutions of further education. The second type included the police and criminal justice organisations.

Contacts with these agencies were important for a number of reasons. Many voluntary agency centres and intermediate treatment schemes received referrals from the courts and social services; centre pupils were themselves frequently involved with social workers, legal counsellors and youth clubs; many centres relied on community resources to complement their programmes.

Staff in most on-site centres relied on regular school channels for community contacts. Staff from educational guidance centres developed contacts primarily with agencies offering medical and psychiatric counselling services. Staff from off-site support centres, voluntary agency centres and intermediate treatment schemes described networks of contacts with such agencies as law centres, the police, careers officers, youth workers, further education institutions and medical and psychological services. Although time-consuming, all staff felt that their pupils greatly benefited from these contacts.

When the centres' links with parents were examined, it was found that most on-site centres had infrequent contact with pupils' parents. The majority of the staff from the remaining centres had regular contact with pupils' families. Parents were invited to visit these centres to discuss pupils' progress and, if necessary, the staff made home visits.

Future Plans
Pupils from half of the voluntary agency centres and two-thirds of the intermediate treatment schemes in this study were not expected to return to their parent schools because of the pupils' age and degree of alienation from school. In these centres preparation for work and opportunities for

work experience were considered to be more relevant than reintegration into school. In all other centres, however, the reintegration of pupils into school was considered very important, particularly so in on-site centres and educational guidance centres which (as previous research has shown)(1) return large proportions of their pupils to mainstream schools.

Most centres followed the same basic reintegration plan, whereby pupils attended school part-time for those classes in which they felt most comfortable. If, for example, a pupil was particularly interested in mathematics, he or she began the reintegration process by attending mathematics lessons at the parent school. The school-based timetable was then gradually increased, one lesson at a time, until the pupil was attending school full-time. If a problem arose in school, the pupil returned to the centre full-time.

This approach necessitated the full co-operation of the school head and classroom teachers. Some centres negotiated the pupil's reintegration plan at the time of referral, in an attempt to ensure school co-operation later on. Many teachers reported that school heads trusted their centres judgment of a pupil's readiness to return and reintegration was not a problem. Others stated that school heads preferred making their own assessments of a pupil's readiness to return, and pupils were interviewed by the headteacher prior to reintegration. Staff from a small number of centres (10 per cent) reported a lack of co-operation from school staff, who did not want pupils to return to school. When centre staff encountered school resistance, they often tried to solve the problem through their management committees.

Pupils were also asked about their own plans for the future. Their responses are shown in Table 6.7.

---

(1) The ILEA monitoring report (Devine, 1980) showed that three-quarters of the pupils leaving on-site secondary centres and over half of those leaving the educational guidance centres returned to their parent schools.

Table 6.7:   Pupils' Plans for the Future.

Plans	Percentage of pupils noting plan N=162
Return to school	48%
Start working	31%
FE college	7%
Remain at centre till school leaving age	7%
Don't know	4%
Other plans(such as travelling)	4%

Almost half the pupils expected to return to school, a third hoped to start working. Seven per cent planned to go to a college of further education and a further 7 per cent planned to remain at their centres until they reached school-leaving age.

When asked whether they were worried about leaving, almost three-quarters of the pupils said they were not. A majority remained non-committal when asked whether they would feel sad or glad at the prospect. Pupils were asked if they had any other plans for their future. Three-quarters commented on the kind of job they would like. Over half of their comments referred to skilled or technical jobs and another 17 per cent mentioned a professional or managerial occupation. The remaining 27 per cent referred to the armed forces, the police, a manual job or 'any' job. Nineteen per cent of the pupils had no plans for the future, and 6 per cent had other plans, such as travelling or living abroad.

Given the employment situation facing these pupils it would appear that their aspirations were somewhat optimistic. Clearly staff, to their credit, had not conveyed low expectations to these young people. However, as a consequence, the chances of pupils being disappointed in the current employment situation are, of course, relatively high.

Summary
Administrative arrangements for the day-to-day running of the centres rested with management committees. The most controversial part of the decision-making process was 'admissions'. Just over half of the centres made their own decisions,

but in the remaining centres admissions were the responsibility of the management committees.

Referral procedures varied, with on-site centres being the least formal; all the other centres had more formal procedures. All off-site centres and two on-site centres met with at least one family member during the referral process.

The collection of information about pupils' educational background was part of the referral process of most centres. Most on-site centres relied on parent school assessment procedures; half of the remaining centres administered formal reading and mathematics tests at the time of admission and just under half assessed pupils' abilities on the basis of work done during the first few weeks.

The curriculum at all centres was designed to duplicate pupils' normal classwork. Many, however, were hampered by lack of specialist teachers and equipment, particularly as far as foreign language and science teaching were concerned. There was often an emphasis on basic instruction and work-oriented training.

The range of teaching styles used included teacher-directed group work, team teaching, individual pupil work programmes and pupil-based group work. Most of the centres supported their teaching with outside activities such as field trips.

Pupils considered that the greatest differences between centres and schools were the good relationships with the centre staff and the atmosphere of the centre. It was apparent from their responses that the pupils liked being at the centres and liked learning English and mathematics. Half the pupils mentioned the academic benefits they obtained from the centres.

Most of the pupils said they had never been away from the centres without a reason. In comparison with their remarks about school absenteeism, it was clear that they were attending centres more regularly than they had been attending school.

One half of the centres appeared to have fairly extensive rules and these were usually very similar to those which exist in most of the mainstream education system. The remaining centres had limited rules which often included more all embracing requirements. The consistency with which rules were applied varied from centre to centre, depending partly on the structure and philosophy of the centre, but more frequently on the personalities of the staff involved.

The practice of a staff member dealing individually with a pupil who was misbehaving appeared to be universal; however, nearly half of the centres also appeared to try and involve the other pupils in censuring unacceptable behaviour in their peers. Three specific strategies were also used to control behaviour - direct confrontation together with sanctions, anticipation and behaviour modification techniques.

Rules noted by most pupils related to smoking - perhaps because this was an activity which often brought pupils into conflict with the staff. When asked what happened when they broke rules the most frequently occurring comments referred to the verbal expression of disapproval by centre staff.

Half of the off-site support centres reported frequent and satisfactory contact with their parent schools. Staff in voluntary agency centres and intermediate treatment schemes were less concerned with parent school relationships, because the pupils in these centres had been out of school for long periods and were not always known to school staff.

Most on-site centre staff relied on regular school channels for community contacts. Staff from off-site support centres, voluntary agency centres and intermediate treatment schemes described networks of contacts with such agencies as law centres, police, careers officers, youth workers, further education, medical and psychological services.

On-site centres had infrequent contact with pupils' parents. The majority of staff from the remaining centres had regular contact with pupils' families.

The same basic reintegration plan was followed by centres, whereby pupils attended school part-time for those classes in which they felt most comfortable. Almost half the pupils expected to return to school and a third hoped to start work.

Chapter 7

SCHOOLS' PERCEPTIONS OF CENTRES

In this chapter, we discuss the information we gathered about the effects of the School Support Programme on the pupils and staff in schools in the ILEA. From our initial contacts with secondary school staff, it became apparent that there were considerable differences between schools in the attitudes and opinions about the support centres held by head teachers. Views on the wide variety of provision included under the auspices of the School Support Programme also differed considerably. We decided, therefore, that a questionnaire should be sent to all ILEA secondary schools at the end of the Autumn term 1980. All 178 questionnaires were returned, but in 36 schools heads were unable to comment on the Programme as they had not used any of the centres. The questionnaire was completed by the headteacher or the senior member of staff having responsibility for the referral of pupils to centres.

There were two main sections to the questionnaire. The aim of the first part was to assess the extent to which schools had used centres during the Autumn term and to enquire as to their demand for centre provision. In the second part we sought to discover the schools' perceptions of the effects of centres on the pupils who attend them, on mainstream pupils, on teachers, and on school management in general. This section of the questionnaire asked for the headteacher's assessments of the benefits and disadvantages of the centres to those involved. It also provided space for some elaboration and qualification of their ratings. Previous discussion with heads suggested that their views were very specific to the centre under discussion. Thus the questionnaire allowed for comments to be made on each centre used by the school.

Schools' use of centres

Heads were asked to identify any centres to which they had sent pupils during Autumn term 1980. The responses are summarised in Table 7.1.

Table 7.1: Centres Used by Schools

Type of centre	Number of schools using each type of centre	Percentage of schools N=178
On-site	42	24%
Off-site support	126	71%
EGC	70	40%
Vol.agcy. centre	35	20%
I.T. scheme	46	26%
Other	24	13%

As can be seen, almost a quarter (24 per cent) of the secondary schools admitted pupils to their own on-site centres, and over two thirds (71 per cent) sent pupils to off-site support centres.

In order to identify any problems associated with referrals to support centres, heads were asked about unsuccessful referrals. Twenty-seven per cent of heads reported unsuccessful referrals – mainly due to a lack of available space, although some inappropriate referrals were made. In some cases there was insufficient time to complete the referral procedures and in others, parents refused to allow their children to attend centres.

Some heads stressed the need for more centre provision:

This school used every available resource fully, but clearly there are still too few places for too many problems.

Our 5th years are ex-grammar school intake, with few problems. Pupils in the on-site centre are 4th years in great need of support. 1981-82 and 1982-83 – much greater need of the centre anticipated with some potentially very difficult 3rd years.

We have so many difficult and demanding pupils
that we need many more such centres if we are
to avoid suspension and exclusion of
alienated, violent pupils. The internal
centres have always helped with the management
of some pupils but they can only deal with a
relatively small number of pupils needing
help.

Heads' Opinions of Centre Effects

Heads were asked to comment on the effects of
centres on pupils sent to them and on teachers and
pupils in mainstream education. Some heads did
not answer the questions because they did not use
any of the centres or because they had not sent
children there for long enough periods to be able
to express opinions about the centre effects.
Answers were received from 142 schools who had used
the centres during the Autumn term.

Centre pupils

This question was answered by 138 heads (97 per
cent of those which used centres). Forty-two per
cent of them described centres as being
'beneficial' without giving any further details.
Others referred to improved attendance and improved
behaviour. The type of comments made by heads are
shown in Table 7.2.

Table 7.2: Beneficial Effects of Centres on
Centre Pupils

Benefits	% of Heads making comment	% of user schools N=142
General beneficial effect	60	42
Improved attendance and punctuality	26	18
Assisted with emotional and behavioural problems	23	16
Facilitated a successful return to school	15	11
Improved work & attitude to school	15	11
Improved behaviour	11	8

Heads most frequently commented on the help
pupils received in off-site support centres and
educational guidance centres with their emotional

and behavioural problems and the improved attendance of pupils who returned from intermediate treatment schemes and voluntary agency centres. The most frequently mentioned benefit of on-site centres was said to be the successful reintegration of pupils.

However, a third of the heads said that, in some cases, the centres had had no effect on the pupils who attended. Some felt the effects had been transitory or that the centres were inappropriate for some pupils. A small number of respondents noted that pupils had not improved their attendance on return to school.

Furthermore, 40 per cent of the heads commented on the 'adverse' effects of centres; a third of these focused on the problems of reintegrating centre pupils into normal lessons. This was mentioned as a problem most frequently by those in schools using on-site and off-site support centres, and was generally thought to result either from the pupil's failure to keep up with school work - especially in practical subjects - or from the lack of pressure in some centres to conform to normal school standards. A third of heads described how the attitudes and behaviour of a few pupils became more difficult following a spell at the centre. This was more likely to be mentioned by heads of schools using off-site support centres than by those using other types of centres and was thought by the heads to be the result of pupils mixing with other 'difficult' pupils in the off-site support centre.

Centre effects on teachers in mainstream education
Ninety-four per cent of the heads of those schools which used centres answered this question. Many of their comments simply described centre effects on mainsteam teachers as 'beneficial' without elaborating on what were the benefits. Table 7.3 shows the most frequently occurring positive comments.

Table 7.3: Beneficial Effects of Centres on Teachers in Mainstream

Benefits	% of heads making comment	% of user schools N=142
Improved classroom management	68	48
Generally beneficial	38	27
Facilitated teaching the rest of the class	34	24
Satisfied with centres' work with centre pupils	21	15
Improved pastoral and discipline arrangements	6	4

Many headteachers (48 per cent) commented on the fact that classroom management became easier and that classroom behaviour had generally improved. Others (34 per cent) pointed out that it was now easier to teach some classes, as the removal of the disruptive children had enabled the teachers to devote all their time to teaching the rest of the class.

However, not all the heads were positive. Over a quarter (27 per cent) of the heads, said that in some cases the centre had not made any difference to teaching in the mainstream classroom. Most of these did not expand further, but a few stated that the pupils at centres 'had not previously attended school anyway' or 'were not disruptive in school'.

Eighteen per cent of the heads commented on the adverse effects of some centres on mainstream teachers. Most of these referred to the difficulty of reintegrating pupils into school - where, for example, work schemes were different or where pupils had gaps in their work as a result of the time spent at the centre. This problem was mentioned by a higher proportion of those using on-site and off-site support centres than of those using other types of centres, possibly because a greater proportion of pupils were reintegrated from these centres. A small number of heads commented on the additional burden of work associated with centres, such as providing work for the pupils in the centre, or following up their attendance. Some commented that the centres allowed teachers to avoid facing problems in the classroom.

Centre effects on pupils in mainstream education
The most frequent comments on the centres' beneficial impact on pupils in mainstream schools are shown in Table 7.4

Table 7.4: Beneficial Effects of Centres on Pupils in Mainstream

Benefits	% of heads making comment	% of user schools N=142
Generally beneficial	51	36
Calmer classroom atmosphere	50	35
Improved working environment	45	36
Improved behaviour and attitudes of mainstream pupils	18	13
Had deterrent effect on other pupils	8	6

Thirty-five per cent of the heads commented on the fact that, in general, pupils were now more settled and that they had better relationships with their teachers. Others (32 per cent) focused on improvements in the working environment and tended to emphasise the fact that pupils in the mainstream were better able to get on with their work without disturbance. Some heads pointed out that there was an improvement in the behaviour of mainstream pupils resulting from the removal of pupils who influenced others to misbehave or truant.

Beneficial effects on mainstream pupils were most frequently reported by heads in relation to off-site support centres and least often with regard to intermediate treatment schemes.

A small proportion of heads (7 per cent) described centres as having little effect on mainstream pupils either because the pupils referred to the centre had not been disruptive or had not been attending school in the first place. A similar proportion of heads indicated that too few pupils had been referred to the centres to make much difference, or that it was too early for the full effect of centre provision to be observed.

Only twelve heads (8 per cent) indicated that centres' effects were adverse. Of these, nine claimed that centres were viewed as a soft option by mainstream pupils. Four commented on the adverse effect of reintegrating centre pupils, whilst two described the guilt felt by mainstream pupils when their classmate was removed to the centre.

Centre effects on school management
The most frequently occurring comments on the beneficial impact of centres on the management of schools are shown in Table 7.5.

Table 7.5: Beneficial Effects of Centres on School Management

Benefits	% of heads making comment	% of user schools N=142
Improved pastoral and discipline arrangements	43	30
Generally beneficial	41	29
Allowed more time for mainstream pupils and other tasks	27	19
Improved behaviour and atmosphere in schools	15	11
Alleviated stress	14	10
Alternative to suspension, expulsion and non-attendance	12	8
Satisfied with centres' work with centre pupils	11	8

Several heads described how the schools' pastoral or disciplinary arrangements had been relieved or improved because of the provision of centres. Others commented on the fact that more time was now available for mainstream pupils and less time was wasted in dealing with difficult pupils. Some heads felt that behaviour and attitudes towards authority and more generally the atmosphere of the school had improved. A few heads felt that centre education was 'better than no education'; that, in other words, the centres provided an alternative to suspension and expulsion.

A minority of heads (14 per cent) felt that centres had had no noticeable effects on school management. Some, pointed out that only a very few pupils were sent to centres and others that it was too early to assess the effects of centres on school management.

Twenty-two per cent of heads, however, felt that the effects on management were adverse. The majority of these described the increase in workload associated with centre provision and some pointed out problems of communication with centres. Only two heads observed that centre provision allowed schools to avoid facing the causes of disruption or non-attendance.

It is, perhaps, not surprising that so few schools criticised centres on the grounds that they enabled the schools to avoid exploring their own contribution to the problem of disruptive behaviour. The centres' very existence is based on the premise that 'disruptive' behaviour can be explained most easily in terms of the individual pupil. As heads were central to the initiation of the School Support Programme it is hardly to be expected that this view would be seriously challenged.

One of the main criticisms of support centres has been the lack of parental rights of appeal against a school's decision to transfer a child to a centre (ACE, 1980). This is seen by critics as contrary to the principles of natural justice. We therefore asked headteachers to describe the reactions of pupils' parents to their child's referral to a centre. It was apparent from the comments that most of the parental reactions were positive. However, 30 per cent of heads of schools that used centres, indicated that some parents were apprehensive or were concerned about the centre's reputation or about removing their child from the mainstream system. Seven per cent of the heads said that some parents were 'unreasonably' negative or blocked referral and a similar number felt that some parents were uninterested or apathetic.

Summary

In order to explore the schools' perceptions of the effects of centres, a questionnaire was sent to the headteachers of all ILEA secondary schools. The first part of the questionnaire was concerned with the schools' use of centres. Twenty-four per cent of the heads stated that they admitted pupils to their own on-site centres and 71 per cent sent pupils to off-site support centres. The second part of the questionnaire was concerned with discovering the schools' perceptions of the effects of centres on the centre pupils, mainstream pupils and teachers and school management in general.

On balance, schools tended to feel that the beneficial effects of the centres tended to outweigh the disadvantages. With regard to the effects of the centres on the pupils who attended them, heads most frequently mentioned the pupils' improved attendance since their return and the assistance they received with emotional and behavioural problems. A considerable number of heads also commented that their schools had benefitted as a result of improvements in overall school management and a calmer atmosphere in the classroom. Staff involved in pastoral and disciplinary procedures were also said to have experienced some relief. On the other hand, for some schools, centres were seen as presenting an additional set of problems. The most frequent complaints were that centres involved school staff in extra work, with the need for lesson preparation for some centre pupils, and with problems of reintegrating centre pupils who had not always been required to conform to ordinary school standards whilst attending the centres.

A few heads commented that the centres had made little impact on their schools either because the numbers of pupils involved were very small or because centre pupils had previously been very irregular attenders.

Chapter 8

EVALUATION

Introduction

The immediate concerns which prompted the research reported in this book can be briefly stated. We wanted to find out whether support centres were of any benefit to the schools and the children who attend them. Conversely, we also wished to know whether centres had any adverse effects on schools, teachers and pupils. Our task, as we saw it, was to answer these seemingly simple questions. It soon became apparent, however, that no simple or quick answers were possible. Indeed, no answers at all could be given without first addressing a whole set of questions about the nature of disruptive behaviour as well as about the organisation and work of the centres. We needed to find out what types of centres were in operation and how they differed from one another; how centres were staffed; what kind of pupils they catered for; how they related to schools, parents and the local community, how the centres were managed; what aims they had and what exactly they did to achieve these; what the relations were between staff and between staff and pupils; and what happened to the pupils when they left.

Each of these factual questions reflected fundamental concerns about the centres and their operation. Do we have the right type and range of support centres? How should they be managed? How should the staff be recruited, organised and supported? What is the best way to liaise with schools, parents and the community? What kinds of children should they cater for? What should be their aims and what are the best ways of achieving them? And, perhaps, ultimately: are centres really necessary or are there better and more efficient ways of dealing with disruptive behaviour; are some types of centre better than others; and do costs vary?

What answers we were able to give to the first set of factual questions we have presented in the preceding seven chapters of this book. In this final chapter we hope, first, to bring together and summarise the most important of our findings and, second, to discuss in the light of these findings, and answer, as far as possible, some of the more fundamental questions and concerns detailed above.

Types of Centres
There are five different types of centres available to ILEA secondary schools: on-site, off-site support, voluntary agency, intermediate treatment and educational guidance centres. The five types could be distinguished by such features as their funding sources, their aims, the types of pupils they were designed to cater for and the pupils' expected length of stay. However, there was also considerable overlap and the overall aims of centres were often noticeably similar. As the centres became more established and gained in experience and understanding, they also tended to be more specific and confident about the sort of pupil behaviour for which they could cater. They also tended to expand the age range of pupils which they felt able to accept and some increased the length of time they considered necessary for the pupil to benefit from the centre programme.

There is, therefore, considerable differentiation between centres and, correspondingly, a wide choice for schools seeking suitable placement for their pupils. However, a differentiated system such as has developed in ILEA is not without its problems. First, there is a pressing need for efficient lines of information and communication between schools (and other referring agencies) and centres, so that the chances of appropriate referrals being made are increased. Second, if they are to benefit fully from their placement outside mainstream schooling, it is vital that the difficulties and needs of pupils to be referred, are correctly assessed before referral. Again, with the rising demand for accountability in education, programme success will, increasingly, need to be demonstrated. It is necessary that evaluation criteria be designed to take full account of the considerable differences between the various types of centres.

None of these problems is insuperable, though we do not, as yet, have any evidence to suggest that they have generally been successfully resolved, either in the ILEA or elsewhere.

What may prove a more intractable problem in the long run is the lack of flexibility and quick response from which any system composed of 'specialist' centres and units is bound to suffer. It can be argued that one of the more important functions of a good support centre system is to provide a readily available alternative for pupils whose relations with their school, have, for whatever reasons, reached a crisis point. What both school and pupil need in such circumstances is an immediate respite from each other for a period of time. If the existing system is such that disruptive pupils cannot be placed until exhaustive assessments have been carried out and suitable centres (with vacancies) found, then both school and pupil will suffer, and their immediate and most pressing problem will remain unresolved.

Pupils in Centres

Almost two-thirds of the pupils referred to the centres were 14 to 16 years old and the remaining one third were 11 to 13 years old. The preponderance of older pupils was particularly noticeable in off-site support centres and voluntary agency centres where they accounted for 70 per cent and 93 per cent of the pupils, respectively. Boys outnumbered girls in all types of centres except the on-site and voluntary agency centres.

Information on the pupils' familial and economic backgrounds was examined and compared with similar information on a sample of pupils from ILEA as a whole. This indicated that pupils in centres were considerably more likely to fall within groups which were socially and economically disadvantaged. This finding is in line with much published research which shows the vulnerability of certain groups of pupils. Within the ILEA, for instance, underachievement has been found to be highly related to social class. (See, for instance, Mortimore & Blackstone, 1982 for a national picture and ILEA, 1983, for a London perspective.)

Because of the concern expressed by local community groups and organisations, such as the Advisory Centre for Education and the Commission for Racial Equality, that ethnic minority pupils might be segregated in support centres, information on ethnic origin was collected. When this information was compared with data from the National Dwelling and Housing Survey (1978) pupils classified as West Indian were found to be slightly over-represented in the centres whereas those classified as 'Indian Sub-Continent' or 'Other' were somewhat under-represented.

Information was also collected on the pupils' academic aims and performance. This indicated that, on transfer to secondary school, a much higher proportion of the pupils was in the lowest Verbal Reasoning group and a lower proportion was in the highest Verbal Reasoning group, when compared with figures for ILEA as a whole. Likewise, the results of the mathematics and reading tests completed by a sample of centre pupils indicated that the majority was performing at a lower level than one would expect for their age. Consequently their examination objectives were somewhat lower than those for ILEA pupils as a whole. Nevertheless more than half the sample reported having some examination objectives.

The main reasons stated for the pupils' referral to centres were 'disruptive' behaviour or non-attendance, or other reasons related to these such as 'bullying' or 'school refusal'. Many of those who were referred to centres on account of 'disruptive' or 'aggressive' behaviour also had a history of problems with school attendance. Over 80 per cent of those referred to voluntary agency centres and intermediate treatment schemes were referred because of absenteeism or school refusal.

These pupil characteristics, detailed above, have important implications for the management and administration of support centres. First, there is the question of the numbers of girls and boys. If some centres contain only one or two girls, this may have serious implications for equal opportunities. For the small proportion of girls who are referred, care must be taken to ensure that their placement is satisfactory and that they are not discriminated against in any of the activities of the centre.

There is, second, the need to maintain an acceptable balance between pupils from different ethnic backgrounds in the centres. Centres where pupils from minority groups preponderate would be unacceptable for both social and educational reasons. We have already referred to fears about the possible segregation of black pupils in support centres. This situation has largely been avoided up to now (to some extent by the conscious decision of support centre staff not to accept large numbers of black pupils) but the danger remains and some formal procedures need to be developed to guard against it. Guidelines for admission could include policy statements on this point, for example, or periodic monitoring could be initiated to monitor this and other aspects of the support centre network.

Third, it is desirable, again for educational reasons, not to isolate any particular age group from younger and older children. Centres, like schools, have to maintain a fairly wide age range. As noted earlier, centres have recognised this and have tried to extend, where possible, the age range of their intake.

It is, similarly, desirable not to limit the intake of any one centre to one 'ability band'. Indeed, as we have seen, the range of pupil abilities was considerable and some pupils were thought capable of a high level of academic achievement. No centre had tried to restrict the range of ability of its intake or to exclude any pupils because they were either backward or very able in some subjects.

On the other hand, both the range of problems for which pupils were referred and the practicalities of maintaining an adequate curriculum and teaching programme point to the need for some 'specialised' units. Although specialisation in terms of behaviour problems dealt with, does not appear extensive - except perhaps for voluntary and intermediate treatment centres which deal primarily with long term absentees and truants - there is a widespread feeling that expertise built up in dealing with particular problems should not be lost or watered down by requiring staff to deal with an over-wide range of behaviour problems. As we noted earlier, this feeling has found expression in the fact that many centres have been refining their aims and criteria for admission, and defining more closely behaviour problems with which they feel they can deal.

We discuss in another section of this chapter the problems and difficulties of supporting adequate curriculum and teaching arrangements at the centres. We should point out here, however, that the curriculum and teaching needs of an intake with a broad age range, wide ability spectrum and multiple behaviour and attendance problems cannot but compound these difficulties and increase the pressure for specialisation.

Management

Apart from on-site centres, which were mostly the responsibility of senior school staff, the formal management of the centres was in the hands of some form of management committee. Management by committee is perhaps the best arrangement for running off-site support and other centres, as so many different interests (local authority, school, centre, pupils, parents, support services and agencies) have to be taken into account and reconciled. Indeed, concern has been expressed that management bodies should include more parents and community representatives.

Senior school staff and management committees varied widely in the range of functions and key decisions which they undertook, or left to the centres' staff. Most management bodies, however, maintained the right to decide on admissions. This is important, for it is particularly with regard to this issue - about who is to be admitted - that the conflicting pressures towards and against specialisation come to a head. Centre staff felt that since centres are designed to cater for pupils with different problems, age ranges and expected lengths of stay, it was important for the success of their programme, to control admissions. On the other hand, management generally believed that, as centres were introduced to serve schools, school heads or management committees should have the final say on admissions.

Although this problem of specialist versus generalist centres, and the associated difficulties of deciding on admission criteria, are likely to be difficult to resolve satisfactorily, broadly based management committees have a better chance than any individual, of maintaining a balance between conflicting interests.

It must be remembered, however, that effective communication and exchange of information between centres and schools (and other agencies and interested bodies) may be more difficult to achieve under a management committee system. Many support centre teachers mentioned the need for better background information and closer co-operation with the schools about the teaching, management and (later on) reintegration into school of children admitted to centres.

Another problem which management by committee may make difficult to avoid (though it also occurs when management is left to senior school staff) has to do with the appointment of new centre staff. Existing centre staff did not always have an opportunity of meeting applicants for vacant posts in their centres before any appointments were made. Staff felt, however, that it was very important to meet prospective members of staff, first, because they would be working in very close co-operation with anyone appointed and they wanted to avoid personality clashes, conflicts and rivalries; and, second, (and perhaps more important) they felt that the centres had little chance of long-term success unless there was considerable agreement among staff about the aims of the centre and the methods by which they could be achieved. As we explain in the next section several centres experienced considerable difficulties because of the lack of consensus among staff about aims and methods.

Aims and Goals

Where problems have occurred in some centres with regard to aims, they have arisen because of lack of clarity in their description and definition, and lack of consensus about them and the methods by which they may be achieved.

The lack of consensus about aims and methods was a serious problem. In about a third of the centres there was little agreement between staff about overall aims and objectives and methods. In a few centres the staff agreed about the overall aims and philosophy of the centre but held independent views about how these should be achieved. Only in about half of the centres was there a general consensus amongst the staff about the overall aims and objectives of the programme, though in many of these one member of staff appeared to be a dominant force in decision-making and it is likely that consensus was in these cases, more apparent than real.

To a large extent, of course, clarity and consensus about aims and methods depend on the relations between the staff, procedures for resolving tension and conflict and for discussing common problems and concerns, and more generally, on the authority structure, organisation and day-to-day running of the centre. (These aspects of centre life are discussed below.) However, clarity and consensus also depend on outside influences and pressures and the expectations that the authority, schools, management committees and others have of the centres. Unless there is a wide measure of agreement between all bodies involved with or having any interest in the centres, the staff, by themselves, stand little chance of establishing a workable, long-term programme. We have already discussed some (and as we shall see there are more) of the conflicts that have emerged about the aims and purposes of support centres. We have also shown that there are many factors and influences which bring about and sustain such conflicts and make, in consequence, any general consensus about aims and goals difficult to achieve.

Where there _is_ general agreement by most of those involved with the support centre scheme, it is about the ultimate destination of centre pupils. It is generally expected that centres should aim at returning pupils to their own schools and help with their reintegration. Nevertheless, the present study found that five out of the nine voluntary agency and intermediate treatment centres in the study were not expecting to return any of their pupils to parent schools because of the pupils' age and degree of alienation from school. These centres tended to concentrate their efforts on preparing their pupils for work and life in the world outside school.

The remaining voluntary agency and intermediate treatment centres and all on-site, off-site support and educational guidance centres aimed at returning pupils to parent schools. In the majority of cases this was a gradual process by which children were first returned to classes and lessons in which they felt more comfortable, and their attendance at school was gradually increased one lesson at a time.

This policy of return and reintegration has three major implications for support centres. First, there is an obvious need for close contacts, exchange of information and co-operation with the referring schools from the moment a child is referred to the centre. There were only a few cases reported where centres experienced what they felt was undue resistance on the part of a school to accept a child back; though of course, as noted earlier, some difficulties were encountered in attempting to establish close links with schools and obtaining detailed background information about pupils referred to centres. (We think reintegration procedures are critically important to the usefulness of centres. However, detailed information on the <u>mechanics</u> of reintegration is not easily obtained. We have already begun a further study of young people who have attended centres and returned to mainstream schooling. In this way we hope to identify good practice amongst both centres and schools.)

Second, there are implications for the curriculum taught in centres. The curriculum must be sufficiently extensive and the syllabus must be tailored to the needs of individual pupils in such a way that, upon return to school, they can fit in with the teaching and activities in their class. As we shall see, this was a difficult problem for support centres, as many of their charges had already fallen behind with their school work long before they came to the centre, and their immediate needs were for remedial teaching in basic subjects, rather than a wide curriculum from which they could not benefit.

Third, the day-to-day life in the centre - methods of teaching, discipline, atmosphere and relations between teachers and pupils - must facilitate return to school, or at least not make it even more difficult for pupils to readjust to ordinary school life.

The need for centre activities to be, in some way, preparatory for return to school is obvious, once stated. What is difficult is to define precisely where the balance should lie between providing an environment which is sufficiently different from school and is perceived by the pupil as a welcome change and a new opportunity (rather than punishment or banishment), which is, at the same time, sufficiently school-oriented to be seen by the pupil as eventually leading to his or her return there. Whether such balance is at all possible will become apparent, we hope, in the more detailed discussion of the relevant issues in the following sections.

Curriculum and Teaching

One of the more serious fears expressed at the outset about support centres was that pupils in centres would be offered a much more limited curriculum than they would receive in a mainstream school and would, consequently also lose the opportunity of entering for public examinations. It was feared, furthermore, that these problems would be complicated and intensified by the wide age and ability ranges found in centres and by the need to duplicate, in any subject taught, the syllabus of the parent school. However, though we did find that centres had to face serious difficulties in this area, the overall picture was by no means as grim as was feared. There were many compensatory developments which should be set against any shortcomings and difficulties - which, if fully developed, should help alleviate many of the current problems.

Obviously curriculum difficulties were not a major problem for on-site centres where most of the pupils' work was set by their own class teachers, and only supervised by the centre's teacher. Similarly, centres which did not consider return to school and reintegration as a first priority, but rather aimed at providing basic instruction and work-oriented training for older pupils who had been out of school for a long time, did not have serious problems or difficulties in maintaining a suitable curriculum.

For other centres, however, curriculum problems were extensive. While basic subjects such as English and mathematics were taught in all centres, the sciences - particularly chemistry - foreign languages, drama and music were available in only a minority of the centres. Specialist resources, text-books and reference material were also rather scarce.

For some pupils attending the centres, these limitations in the range of subjects available and teaching resources were of little real consequence. These pupils had not benefited from the mainstream syllabus, in any case, and centre staff therefore concentrated on teaching and improving basic skills. For other pupils such limitations were obviously of somewhat greater importance.

From the point of view of centre management and staff, the difficulties involved were, first, in finding staff qualified and experienced in specialist subjects; and second, difficulties arising from the need to duplicate school courses. This was a particularly thorny problem when centres accepted pupils from many schools (in some centres, up to ten schools at a time), and many centres had to approximate to, rather than duplicate, mainstream curricula.

It is interesting to consider the implications of these findings for some of the issues which were raised and discussed in previous sections. It is obvious, for example, that if centres restricted their intake to pupils from one or two schools, many of these curriculum difficulties would be obviated. It is easier to duplicate the courses of one or two schools rather than ten. It is also easier to establish close contacts and co-operation with a small number of schools. Such close links may enable centres to draw more extensively on the schools' teaching resources and expertise to supplement their own. It should be noted, however, that restricting the intake of centres to one or two schools would necessitate a 'generalist' rather than a 'specialist' approach, as otherwise those centres involved would not have a viable intake.

There are, of course, other possible solutions to curriculum problems that are worth exploring (and which may be more compatible with the 'specialist' centre approach). For example, further consideration could perhaps be given to establishing teacher resource centres, with special responsibilities for support staff, in order to assist in the provision of learning materials and equipment and to foster relationships between staff (and possibly pupils) from different centres, though such developments would increase the cost of provision. Again, arrangements should continue to be made to enable centre staff to meet together to discuss ways in which they might develop their curriculum and to exchange information on relevant teaching methods and innovative techniques. Such initiatives may prove very useful, and indeed, they appear to be bearing fruit even in the limited instances where they have been tried. However, even if completely successful, they would not diminish the great need for closer links between school and centre. The need for constant exchange of information and co-operation about the pupils, about the school curriculum and about the process and progress of reintegration, would remain.

Whatever the limitations of the curriculum and the teaching difficulties experienced by centre staff and pupils, it should not be forgotten that in many ways centres are better placed than schools to introduce new subjects. They are also well placed to adopt new approaches to teaching, and generally to pay more attention to individual pupils, help them overcome personal problems, develop study and social skills, and encourage self-management.

Subjects and activities introduced by centres included interior decorating, motor mechanics, office and clerical skills (mostly with immediate practical experience). Extra-curricular activities included outings for the pupils to museums, recreational centres and sporting events. Such activities were seen by the staff as providing training in self-management and social skills.

Novel teaching and training techniques used by centre staff included role-modelling, group work and methods for changing behaviour based on concepts borrowed from social psychology. For example, some centres organised their work around group sessions where staff and pupils had (at least in theory) an equal say in making decisions about rules and sanctions and in planning future activities.

There is little doubt that pupils can gain extensive benefits from a novel and flexible programme with more personal attention and with new opportunities, subjects, activities and training techniques. New experiences offered by centres will, hopefully, help their pupils acquire viable study skills, social skills, self-confidence and interest in their work. The difficult question to answer is not whether such programmes are worthwhile, but rather to what extent the experiences they provide are preparatory to, or at least not incompatible with, successful reintegration into mainstream schooling.

There may be little justification, for instance, in starting pupils on new subjects and activities if these cannot be further pursued once they return to the mainstream schools. The new experiences, may also, result in pupils becoming less conformist and, although they may have developed in various ways, they may find a return to school a difficult experience. Furthermore, the actual nature and direct effects of centre life and activities on the pupil are only one set of factors influencing reintegration. Another set of powerful influences on the success of reintegration depends on the way the centres and their activities are presented to the pupils concerned by school and centre staff, and more particularly, on how pupils themselves perceive them. We return to these questions later on, but should point out here that what is ideally needed is for pupils to view centres in a positive light, that is, they must not consider their time there either as punishment or banishment, if they are to gain maximum benefit from their stay. At the same time pupils must not think of the centre as a soft option or permanent escape from school. So long as the return to mainstream schools remains the ultimate aim, pupils must view the centre as primarily offering a preparation for their return.

Staff-Pupil relations, Controls and Sanctions

Two further areas of centre life which were selected for observation and analysis were the relationships between staff and pupils and the atmosphere in the centres. These two features are closely related to those just discussed and have also been previously highlighted in the literature as of particular importance in relation to the education of pupils with behavioural difficulties. The pupils were primarily at the centres because of a breakdown in the relationship with their parent school and consequently the staff were acutely aware of the need to create rewarding relationships with them to enable learning to take place.

Teachers throughout the education system face a dilemma about the extent to which they should become involved with their pupils' personal and family problems. Teachers in centres, however, felt this dilemma even more acutely as their pupils' personal difficulties were often such as to place a serious obstacle in the path of formal learning. The response of centre staff varied considerably from those who felt that the centres' task was predominantly to educate (the apparent philosophy of approximately half the centres) to those who thought that this was impossible without offering considerable assistance with personal and home problems (approximately a quarter of the centres).

It was obviously not possible to consider all components of the inter-relationship between staff and pupils or to describe all the characteristics of the prevailing atmosphere or tone in the centres. The two key dimensions which became apparent during the analysis were the extent to which the staff and pupil relationships were formally structured and the degree of comfort or strain that existed in the day-to-day working of these structures. The majority of centres appeared to have an organised structure to their staff/pupil relationships, but within this framework, were able to function, for at least some of the time, in a relaxed and informal fashion. The study team were impressed by the extent to which many of the centre staff had developed rapport with their pupils and had established a climate where effective teaching could occur.

The staff at the centres felt that maintaining such a constructive relationship with pupils in a relaxed atmosphere depended, largely, on the extent to which they (the staff) were able, to determine the number and kind of pupils they would admit to their support centre and ensure that those admitted were not completely at odds with pupils already there in terms of their personality and temperament. This is a powerful argument, both for allowing centres to limit their intake (but not necessarily to one type of pupil) and to have a strong say on who is to be admitted to the centre.

Of course, even in the most relaxed and easy of circumstances it is necessary to ensure that rules are observed and order maintained if work is not to be interrupted and disrupted. The specific techniques used by the staff to control behaviour included the use of the pupil group censuring the pupils within it (a technique which is also reported as prevalent in schools for the maladjusted); behaviour modification based primarily on the use of rewards; direct confrontation backed by a variety of sanctions ranging from the withdrawal of privileges to temporary exclusion from the centre, and parental involvement.

The question of the compatibility of the centre atmosphere and staff-pupil relations with the pupils' eventual return to mainstream schooling and reintegration must be raised again. It would appear that similar considerations apply: to the extent that these aspects of centre life bolster self-confidence, foster skills and solve personality problems they are helpful to reintegration; to the extent that they make centre life appear an easy option or a preferable alternative to school, they hinder reintegration.

Staff Organisation and Duties

Several concerns relating to the staff in the centres, which were previously reported in the literature, have also been highlighted in the present study. These included the range of duties attached to the teaching posts, the demanding nature of the work and the need to work outside school hours to complete administrative tasks.

The centre teachers in the present study reported that apart from their teaching duties and lesson planning they had responsibility for centre and programme administration, such as organising meetings, preparing reports and arranging for guest speakers. They were also involved in parent school and community liaison work, clerical duties, counselling support to pupils, meal preparation, cleaning and centre maintenance chores. Not surprisingly, the majority of staff and especially the teachers-in-charge reported that it was necessary for them to spend a considerable amount of their own time on centre duties. Centre staff, therefore, felt that they needed help with their clerical and domestic duties and the flexibility of hiring specialist staff on a sessional basis. They also asked that the centre programme should be arranged to allow for staff to have some time for relaxation during the school day.

Previous literature has indicated the importance of staff relationships in schools which cater for disturbed pupils. During this study attempts were made, therefore, to describe the authority structure within centres and the relationships between the staff.

In their day-to-day life and activities, over one third of the centres appeared to be run on predominantly democratic lines, with decision-making often being the responsibility of all or most of the staff. In many of these centres procedures were established for making decisions, such as specific group meetings to discuss aims and policy on referrals. Most of the other centres studied, were run on lines which were partly formal and hierarchical, and partly democratic. Only one of the centres could be described as strictly hierarchical in organisation with decisions taken without discussion or consultation between staff.

In general, the staff appeared to be most relaxed within a formal structure where it was obvious who had the ultimate reponsibility and power. Within that basic framework, however, it appeared that where centres were organised on the basis of established democratic procedures and the staff genuinely participated in decision-making, there also appeared to be a higher level of staff involvement in their work and commitment to its success.

As noted earlier, however, good relations within the centres also depend on a number of extraneous factors and circumstances, such as the judicious selection of staff and pupils and the number and range of behaviour problems the pupils bring with them. Furthermore, harmonious relationships depend to a large extent, on the degree of consensus among staff about the aims of the centre and methods of achieving them although, of course, as we have already explained, consensus itself partly depends on, and presupposes good relations among staff and adequate opportunities for discussing issues, problems and difficulties, and for resolving conflict and tension.

Links with Schools, Parents and Community Agencies

We have already mentioned several times the need for close links with schools, both for the benefit of individual pupils and for the long-term interests and efficient running of support centres. However, as all centres, especially 'off-site' centres are separate organisational units they also depend on effective relationships with community agencies and pupils' families to operate their programmes successfully. Much of the opposition to centres and especially to 'off-site' centres has focused on the possibility that pupils attending them would become isolated and segregated from the mainstream educational system and that their families and community agencies would not be sufficiently involved in the management, organisation or educational programme of these centres. We reviewed, therefore, the type and frequency of contacts between centres (excluding the on-sites) and their parent schools. We also investigated the links between all centres (both on-site and 'off-site') and other community agencies together with the relationships which existed between centres and the pupils' families.

The various types of centre were found to differ somewhat in the extent of their contact with parent schools. Educational guidance centres as a whole appeared to have established the most extensive contacts with schools and were more often satisfied with the relationships which had developed, whereas amongst the off-site support centre staff, the extent of satisfaction expressed regarding parent school contacts was more variable. In general, staff in voluntary agency and intermediate treatment centres were less concerned with parent school relationships because these centres' pupils had been out of school for long periods and were not known to school staff.

The factors which were thought to contribute to poor relationships where these existed, between centre staff and parent schools, included the centre's location, disagreement and misunderstandings about the centre's objectives, inappropriate referrals and a lack of staff time.

The study team felt that parent schools could perhaps involve centre staff more in the life and work of their schools and provide them with opportunities for explaining to school staff the centre's aims and programmes. It would probably be necessary, however, to provide the centre with some additional staff resources to enable the centre staff to participate to any greater extent in parent school activities.

There were two types of community agencies with which support centres had frequent contact. One type was the 'helping' agencies such as social and family services, medical clinics, job counselling and placement agencies and institutions of further education. The second type included law enforcement and criminal justice organisations. On-site centre staff more frequently relied on regular school channels for community contacts, while staff from all other centres described networks of contacts with such agencies as law centres, and police, with industry and with further education, medical and psychological services. Although time-consuming, all staff felt that their pupils greatly benefited from these contacts.

When the study team reviewed the contacts between centre staff and pupils' families it was found that, as with community agency contacts, most on-site centres had infrequent contact with pupils' parents. Again, these teachers relied mostly on school pastoral care staff. However, almost three-quarters of all the other centres were found to have regular contact with pupils' families, while the remainder reported having only 'intermittent' contact, usually at a time of crisis or when a pupil was absent from the centre without explanation.

Links with parents and, through them, the local community are important for both the individual children involved and, more generally, for the long-term success of support centres. Parents must be convinced that attendance at the centres is not some form of punishment or exclusion, but of benefit to the child. A spell at a support centre must not be seen as a stigma by the community, peers and neighbours, leading to some form of labelling for the child, but rather as a constructive, even if unusual, step in his or her education. Obviously, these considerations lead back, once more, to the question of what centres are for, their aims objectives and methods. Some general agreement about these issues is necessary, for each centre (and parent school) and for the support centre system as a whole, if a coherent and acceptable image and good reputation for support centres is to be maintained in the community, among parents and among pupils.

Effect and Outcome for Pupils

There was considerable evidence to suggest that pupils attending centres had a fairly well-balanced view of the centres. That is, most pupils saw centres in a positive light, but at the same time, they were not over-attached or over-dependent on them. (As we explained earlier such a balanced range of attitudes is necessary if centres are to help pupils overcome any problems they have and to reintegrate them into mainstream schooling.)

Approximately 60 per cent of the pupils interviewed indicated that their initial reactions to referral were positive. They were favourably impressed by their preparatory visits to the centre and saw their referral largely as 'an opportunity to do well'. Again, when asked about life at the centre most pupils had some positive comments to make, usually about the general atmosphere of the centres, staff, conditions of work and the range of activities.

The generally positive feelings that pupils had about attending the centres were reflected in their attitudes to being absent without reason. Seventy per cent of them said that they had never been absent without reason, and most of the remaining 30 per cent said they had stayed away only occasionally.

At the same time pupils were, on the whole, quite realistic about their stay in the centre. Nearly 50 per cent of them expected to return to their schools after a spell at the centre and another 7 per cent expected to go to further education colleges. Most of those who did not expect to return to mainstream schools were older children attending centres where the policy was to prepare for work and adult life rather than school.

This balanced range of views, feelings and experiences was encouraging. However, it must not be forgotten that there were some disturbing findings. Approximately, 22 per cent of the pupils were rather indifferent to their referral: they did not care whether they attended school or a support centre. Another 22 per cent viewed their referral with some apprehension. They appeared to be most concerned about the centres' reputation, about being separated from their friends, or simply about how they would cope with a new place. There were also some negative comments about life at the centres, though these were usually made by less than 10 per cent of the pupils. These included dislike of other pupils, dislike of facilities or location and dislike of centre teachers or the curriculum. Nevertheless, most pupils liked attending the centres (in spite of some negative comments). Only 4 per cent of the pupils interviewed indicated that they disliked the centres and a further 8 per cent were non-committal. More disturbing, perhaps, was the minority of pupils who did not dislike the centres, but saw them only as an escape from school or as a softer option offering them 'more freedom'.

The vast majority of pupils not only liked attending the centres but also felt that they were benefiting from their stay there. More than half of them emphasised the academic progress they were making, especially in basic subjects, and another quarter mentioned that they were learning to cope with their own problems. About 20 per cent of them commented that the centre was helping them to readjust and reintegrate into their own school. Only 7 per cent of the pupils felt that there were no benefits to be gained from attending a support centre.

Information from the schools which had used support centres for some of their pupils tended to confirm that children were, on the whole, benefiting from their attendance there. Heads mentioned improved attendance and punctuality among pupils, improved behaviour, emotional stability and generally better attitudes to work and school. Many schools also commented on the successful reintegration of pupils attending centres. On the other hand, a number of heads expressed reservations about the effectiveness of centres. They felt that, in some cases, centres had no effect, or only transitory effects on the pupils who attended them. Some heads even felt that effects on mainstream pupils were on the whole adverse, as pupils tended to view centres as 'soft options', or because of difficulties in reintegrating returning pupils.

Effects and Outcomes for Schools
The information discussed in the previous section about the centres' effects on pupils who attended them, came from a questionnaire which all ILEA

secondary schools completed for us during the Autumn term of 1980. Apart from their views on centre pupils, schools were asked for comments on the effects of centres on mainstream pupils and teachers, and on school management in general. They were also requested to give us details about their use of, and demand for, centre places.

One fifth of secondary heads said they had never used support centres. The remaining schools referred approximately 1,900 pupils to centres during the Autumn term, an average of 13 pupils per school. Only 27 per cent of the schools reported unsuccessful referrals. These were due to lack of space at the centres, inappropriate referrals, parents' refusal and lack of time to complete referral procedures.

Approximately 40 per cent of the schools which used centres could be said to be overwhelmingly positive in their attitudes towards the centres; their comments showed that in their view the effects of the centres were beneficial in all areas and on all pupils and staff concerned. The remaining heads, though on the whole positive in their attitudes, did make a variety of negative comments in relation to one or more of the effects of the centres.

Apart from comments on centre pupils, which we have already discussed, many heads commented on the fact that centre provision allowed them to improve classroom management, teaching arrangements for the rest of the class and pastoral care. Some heads commented on the generally improved atmosphere in the school and a few expressed the view that support centres provided a valuable alternative to suspension and expulsion. On the other hand, about 13 per cent of the heads who made use of centres mentioned the additional workload involved, such as providing extra work for the pupil while at the centre and while the pupil was being reintegrated into school. A few heads felt that centre provision allowed schools and teachers to avoid facing the root causes of disruption and non-attendance.

In general, it would seem that the majority of schools appreciated the support being provided by the centres and perceived their impact on school life as being mostly positive. Where close communication between centres and schools had been established, it also appeared that both sides benefited from the exchange of ideas and techniques for dealing with pupils whose behaviour is seen as a threat to the orderly functioning of the group.

Effects and Outcomes for Centre Teachers

The establishment of centres, separate from the mainstream educational system, has given rise to concern not only for the pupils who attend but for the teachers who are employed there. This concern has mainly been focused on three aspects of their teaching situation: on the degree of professional support received and day-to-day contact with other teaching staff; on the opportunities for in-service training; and on the long term opportunities for career advancement.

When questioned regarding the effects of the teaching situation on their personal and professional lives, approximately one half of the teachers-in-charge, directors and other teachers interviewed said they did not feel in anyway professionally isolated in the centres. They felt they were part of a school (especially if they were in an on-site centre), they had numerous outside contacts, they attended training courses and they had the support of other teachers in the centre. However, 12 per cent of the teachers felt isolated on occasion, and the remaining 38 per cent said that they definitely suffered professional isolation. These teachers felt that they did not have sufficient contact with others, their own role was not adequately defined, and they lacked the stimulation of a school setting and professional tradition. A variety of measures can be taken to alleviate such problems. These include the expansion of national and local facilities for in-service training and an advisory service; the interchangeability of staff between centres and ordinary schools; the integration of centre staff into the overall planning processes of schools; and the continual recognition by the teaching profession as a whole of their collective responsibility for difficult pupils.

In-service training was seen by the teachers as important in providing opportunities for learning relevant teaching methods and pursuing their professional concerns. Only 20 per cent viewed their training opportunities as adequate. The rest felt that there were no training courses readily available to them that were directly relevant to support centre teaching, or, that given the limited staffing arrangements at the centres, it was not possible for them to take time off for training. Nevertheless, more than half of the teachers had attended one or more courses - usually part-time degree or diploma courses.

For many of the teachers, accepting a post within a support centre had resulted in a promotion, while for others it had been a transfer at the same level and, for a minority, the post was at a lower level than their previous one. Those teachers not promoted on entry reported other professional benefits, such as the pleasure of teaching an interesting group of pupils and the innovative and independent nature of the work.

Teachers in on-site centres, in general, did not feel that their careers had been adversely affected by teaching in centres. Most of them expected to advance professionally by moving into a counselling or pastoral care post or by becoming 'head of year'. Teachers in all other types of centres felt that their career advancement was a problem. Teachers-in-charge and directors of centres were particularly concerned that they would not be considered for high-level posts in schools because of their absence from mainstream education. Other teachers though concerned, were on the whole, less pessimistic about their opportunities for advancement. Most of them hoped to advance to a higher post within their own or another centre, while some expected to return to mainstream education, pursue other careers such as counselling, or return to university. Some previous studies have also reported that many teachers in centres are concerned about their career prospects, working as they do outside the mainstream educational system, while other writers have warned of the danger of creating a new category of specialist teachers.

Two further issues need to be discussed.

On-site versus 'off-site' centres
Throughout this book we have drawn attention to differences between the various types of centres. The intermediate treatment schemes and, to a certain extent, the voluntary agency centres are inevitably different, partly funded and supervised, as they are, from various sources and dealing with particular kinds of pupils. However, the on-site centres, off-site support centres and the educational guidance centres have more in common. Though we have drawn attention to the increasing specialisation of types of centres we are also aware that this has occurred primarily because the

existence of a range of provision has allowed it to do so. In this section we will consider the advantages and disadvantages that, from our analysis, different types of centres appear to have.

On-site centres

There appear to us to be three major advantages for the pupils: easier access, more continuity of teaching and curriculum and easier reintegration into the mainstream. Access is obviously made easier through informal teacher communication. The centre's location within the school enables referral to be seen as a change of class or course rather than the more fundamental transfer to an 'off-site' centre. For many pupils attendance at the on-site centre was only part-time. Practical lessons, games and subjects which provided less opportunity for disruptive behaviour could still be attended.

Part-time attendance clearly aided the maintenance of continuity for pupils. Similarly, on-site provision enabled pupils to follow more closely the same curriculum as their peers, with work being sent to the centre and feedback being given to the subject teacher via the support-team. Where possible the opportunity to continue laboratory and workshop sessions was taken.

Reintegration is also easier when pupils have remained on-site and especially when their attendance at centres has been on a part-time basis. A move to full-time mainstream classes that is judged to be premature can be rectified far more easily than if a change of sites is involved.

Against these clear advantages must be set out the following disadvantages: change is only partial, the overall ethos of the institution remains constant, and a 'fresh start' is less feasible. For some pupils, relations with peers or with teachers may have sunk to such a state that the move to an on-site centre may not be sufficient for the pupils to feel they can make a fresh start. Even though the centre teacher may be new to the pupil, he or she may be associated in the mind of the pupil with teachers in the mainsteam.

There is also the danger that the centre may become a ghetto within the school. Although opportunity for part-time attendance in the mainstream may exist, centre pupils may cling to the security of their small unit and it may be rejected. An additional problem is that some centres might be viewed as 'punishment' centres by teachers and pupils alike; such a view is not helpful to pupils already alienated from the school.

There are also a number of advantages for the staff of on-site centres. We have commented earlier on the feelings of isolation that were reported to us by teachers working in off-site centres. Clearly, on-site centres offer the opportunity to avoid this. Furthermore, it is obviously easier to provide cover for staff illness or attendance at in-service courses. Finally, because there need not be a total commitment to the centres by the teachers, some mainstream teaching can be continued and career opportunities in either centres or ordinary schools can be pursued.

However, just as there were some disadvantages for pupils so there are for teachers. The location of the centre within the school may inhibit innovative methods. The experiments involving pupils in the management of the centres, that we have noted earlier, are not as feasible in on-site as in 'off-site' provision. Even though school rules may be modified within the centre, both pupils and teachers will be subject to the general jurisdiction of the school.

There are then both advantages and disadvantages for pupils and teachers in the use of on-site centres. It may be that some pupils and teachers will be more suited to on-site and others to 'off-site' provision.

There are also four other advantages. First, the response to disruptive behaviour can be much faster. Even though a centre may not be able to function as an emergency 'cooling-off' unit and cater for pupils for longer periods, where staff are colleagues and where management is common, delay can be reduced to a minimum. Second, and perhaps more importantly, the school is unable to 'banish' its pupils. Difficulties which arise in the school also have to be resolved within the school. Furthermore, the presence of the support centre teachers on the school staff provides formal and informal opportunities to act as advocates of vulnerable pupils. Given the discussion of disruptive behaviour with which we began this book (and its emphasis on pupil, teacher and school influences) the existence of such advocates may be important. Third, the cost to the LEA of on-site provision is considerably less than that of off-site centres as will be discussed in a later

section. Finally, on-site provision is in tune
with a post-Warnock philosophy of special
educational need.

'Off-site' centres

Some of the advantages of off-site centres have
already been noted in the previous section.
Briefly these may be summarised as follows: they
allow pupils a real change from the school in which
they have been unsuccessful, and they allow
teachers freedom to experiment with innovatory
educational methods. In addition, we have
identified other advantages such as the higher
level of parental involvement and communications
found in off-site centres and the impressive
dedication of teachers that led to out-of-hours
activities, holidays and many other ways of helping
pupils who, for whatever reason, had found their
ordinary schooling to be a negative experience.

Paradoxically, the principal disadvantage of
off-site centres appears to us to be the very
separateness that we have already claimed enabled
the centres to function so well. In our view some
of the off-site centres we studied can also be seen
as models of alternative schools. As such they
bear little relation to the mainstream they
ostensibly serve. Aims and objectives are very
different as are the organisation, rules,
expectations and ethos.

We wish to stress that we were, in general,
very impressed by these centres and by their
teachers who had so often enabled pupils with a
history of failure and unhappiness to achieve
success. The reservations that we have concern the
practical difficulty of reintegration following a
sustained spell at such a centre and the danger
that mainstream schools remain unaffected by these
developments. In other words, off-site centres can
provide a dumping ground for difficult pupils and
schools can be spared the need to take
responsibility for disruptive behaviour.

Educational Guidance Centres

Educational guidance centres were distinguished
from other types of centres mainly by their links
with the schools psychological service. Incoming
pupils had been thoroughly screened and specialist
advice and support was always available. As we
have noted earlier, these centres also achieved
strong links with parents. Although they were
sited away from schools, their connections with the

schools psychological service prevented teachers from feeling too isolated and enabled in-service training to take place. Furthermore, the issue - to which we have referred in previous sections - of the control of admissions did not apply to educational guidance centres since this fell to the responsibility of the local educational psychologist.

In some ways, therefore, this type of centre provide a model of an off-site support centre which can cater for pupils who have experienced difficulities in adjusting to ordinary school. They form a mid-point between special educational provision (such as schools for the maladjusted) and on-site support centres.

Comparative costs of centres

Even though thorough financial breakdown of different kinds of provision was beyond the scope of our study, we could not ignore the question of costs (for a study of cost effectiveness see Topping, 1983). The overall sum of money initially allocated to the ILEA programme was £1.6 million. In this section we shall discuss the comparative costs of the different types of centre.

The cost of on-site centres, in general, is limited to the cost of the staff since accommodation and services (such as heating, lighting and telephone charges) will be included as part of the costs of the parent school. In addition, there will, of course, be books, paper, educational equipment and other material but these are likely to represent only a very small proportion of the school's budget.

In contrast, all off-site provision of whatever type (off-site support centres, educational guidance centres, voluntary agency centres or intermediate treatment schemes) is likely to be more expensive since the costs of accommodation and services will have to be met. Furthermore, there are likely to be initial extra costs as the buildings - usually disused schools - are converted for use as centres.

There are two other obvious points to be made about costs. First, where attendance at a centre is on a part-time basis and there is a regular through-flow of pupils the cost per pupil (unit cost) will be considerably less than if pupils are full-time and remain in the centres for long periods. Second, the unit cost will be much less if all available places are filled, than if spare places are left empty. Yet inevitably there are times in the year when there may be a lack of suitable referrals. Thus at the beginning of the school year, teachers are likely to be reluctant to refer pupils to centres and may well delay doing so until later in the term when alternative measures have been tried. This practice is educationally sound, yet if expensive staff at centres are under used, may not make financial sense. In cases such as this, on-site provision may prove economically superior since staff could spend their time working in other parts of the parent school. Staff in off-site support centres who have a commitment to several schools find this less feasible.

Conclusion

As we have seen the ILEA School Support Programme offers considerable direct and immediate benefits for pupils, teachers and schools. It is, furthermore, possible to argue that the Programme is providing the potential for useful reforms within the mainstream educational system. Throughout this study a variety of innovative approaches to teaching have been found. Some staff were experimenting with organising their decision-making process on a more democratic basis than is usually found in the mainstream system. In addition, centre staff were found to be meeting together, informally and forming groups such as LEAP (London Educational Alternatives Programme). Within these groups there is discussion as to what the educational and social aims of their centres should be, their methods of work and organisation, and the ways of establishing a constitution to protect the rights of pupils and parents and to involve the whole community in the educational process. The new approaches to education which are being explored in centres are perhaps the most forceful argument in favour of the School Support Programme, namely that it may provide an opportunity for a new look at the process of schooling.

Turning to the disadvantages associated with attendance at support centres, we have identified a number of serious concerns. These arose mainly from difficulties with the curriculum which prevent pupils from pursuing a wide range of subjects and examination objectives and may, upon return to school, hinder the pupils' reintegration into school. Furthermore, we have already discussed the danger that centres may be seen by some teachers as an opportunity to avoid facing up to those problems created by the ethos of the school. If it were to become established practice that pupils who showed difficulties could be banished to a centre without a proper examination of the reasons for referral, then the dangers of centres would be very serious. Headteachers and teachers-in-charge must, therefore, exercise great caution over which pupils, and for what reasons pupils are referred to centres.

On the other hand, as we have seen, centres faced a considerable number of problems and potential dangers associated with their reputation and standing among pupils and the wider community, their management, staff recruitment, workload and relations with schools. Many of these difficulties were still unresolved at the time of the study, though the beginnings of solutions were emerging in some areas and suggestions for further steps and initiatives were forthcoming in relation to other areas. What form any solutions which are finally adopted, will take, is impossible to say on present evidence. It does appear certain, however, that most of the problems faced by centres can only be contained or resolved by firm guidance, planning, support and assistance from the central authorities involved. Solutions, in other words, must be system-wide.

This is particularly true of the problem of 'specialisation', that is the degree to which groups of centres or individual units, may tailor or limit their intake in terms of behaviour problems, personality traits, age, ability and ethnic background. There is, as we noted, a measure of agreement about the degree of specialisation in terms of some of these factors, but by no means about all. Problems are particularly acute in relation to the range of behavioural difficulties that centres can tackle, in deciding which individual children are best suited for admission (i.e., individuals who will not disrupt the life and work of other pupils already admitted) and, in consequence, in relation to the aims, objectives and methods employed by centres. These disagreements arise, as we have seen, from a wide range of conflicting pressures and circumstances both from within and outside centres. Because of this, lasting solutions will be difficult to work out, but are likely to involve detailed system-wide planning resulting in a workable balance of 'on-site' and 'off-site' centres, with, perhaps some of the latter run on 'on-site' lines, that is, accepting immediate referrals and acting as agents of parent schools, supervising work set by staff from the referring schools and so on. The question of whether one type of centre is superior to others is difficult to answer as has been shown earlier.

There remains only one major question to consider before closing this chapter. Are support centre schemes an adequate answer to disruptive behaviour in schools, or are there better and more efficient methods of dealing with the problem? The answer, of course, on the evidence presented here can only be a tentative and qualified 'yes' in favour of support centres. As we have seen, support centres appear to be of benefit and there are, at least, possibilities of reducing problems associated with them to manageable proportions. A more definite judgment can only be made when such initiatives and possible solutions to problems as have been started or suggested, have been actually developed and tried out; and when concrete evidence has been collected and presented about the efficacy of alternative ways of dealing with disruption in inner city schools.

There are three main approaches to the problem of disruptive behaviour suggested by educationalists. First, it is suggested that additional support and resources (such as the peripatetic support teacher teams discussed earlier) should be made available to all schools. Second, it is argued that the curriculum and examination system should be reappraised and adjusted so that mainstream schools can become more responsive and flexible, and better able to cater for the needs of all their pupils, without recourse to support centres or other outside agencies. Third, some educationalists go even further and suggest that funds should be made available for developing alternative schools. These schools like those found in the United States, it is suggested, would allow for the development of local initiatives and innovations and would be able to pioneer new approaches to education which may ultimately influence the mainstream system. This, it is thought, would allow for a greater degree of choice for individual children and their parents.

We would, of course, not condemn, or dismiss such approaches. Indeed, as we have already pointed out evidence from the self-evaluation exercise of the support team of peripatetic teachers demonstrates the efficiency of such an approach (Coulby & Harper, 1981).

As to the question of the reform of secondary education, we are firmly of the opinion that considerable change is long overdue. The current system of secondary education, in our judgment, allows public examinations to dominate the curriculum and organisation of schools. Teachers as much as pupils are constrained and there is the evidence that we have already presented that pupils referred to centres for behavioural problems are in most need of academic help. This is clearly not the place for a detailed discussion of the examination system and its effects on pupils (see Mortimore & Mortimore, 1983, for a view of this area) yet we cannot ignore the impact of the system upon the behaviour of pupils and upon the working of teachers.

We are less convinced of the arguments for the development of 'alternative' schools. In our view the reform of examinations and the revision of the secondary curriculum would allow schools such flexibility that 'alternative' schools would not be necessary.

In an ideal education system - where all pupils were highly motivated and where misbehaviour was uncommon - there would be little need for the centres we have described in this study. Until our present system approaches more closely to the ideal, however, there is likely to remain the need for some form of centre provision. Those responsible for education must, therefore, find ways of limiting the dangers associated with centres and of building on the pioneering efforts of the teachers we have described.

BIBLIOGRAPHY

ADVISORY CENTRE FOR EDUCATION (1980) Disruptive
    units: labelling a new generation. Where,
    158, May 1980.

ADVISORY CENTRE FOR EDUCATION SURVEY (1980)
    Disruptive units. Where, 158, May 1980.

ADVISORY CENTRE FOR EDUCATION (1982) Suspension.
    Where, 179, June 1982.

ALHADEFF, G., GREENHALGH, P., MORGAN, G and PEACY,
    N. (1982) Separate development. Times
    Educational Supplement, 9 July 1982.

ALLEN, R. and GLADSTONE, F. (1980) Alternative
    Education. Voluntary Action pp 18-20, Autumn
    1980.

BAILEY, J.S. (1982) Special units in secondary
    schools. Educational Review, 34, No. 2.

BASINI, A. (1981) Urban Schools and 'disruptive
    pupils': a study of some ILEA support units.
    Educational Review, 33, No. 3.

BENNETT, N. (1976) Teaching Styles and Pupil
    Progress. London: Open Books.

BERG, I. (1980) Absence from school and the law.
    In Hersov, L. and Berg, I. (eds). Out of
    School. Chichester: John Wiley.

BERGER, A. and MITCHELL, G. (1978) Multitude of sin
    bins. Times Educational Supplement, 7 July
    1978.

141

Bibliography

BERGER, M., YULE, W. and WIGLEY, V. (1980) Intervening in the classroom. Contact, ILEA, 12 September 1980.

BIRD, C., CHESSUM, R., FURLONG, J. and JOHNSON, D. (eds) (1980) Disaffected Pupils. Brunel University, Educational Studies Unit.

BOLTON, E. (1981) Disruptive pupils. In Evans, M. (ed) Disruptive Pupils. London: Schools Council Publications.

BRIAULT, E. (1975) Educational administration and the contemporary city. In Hughes, M. (ed) Administering Education: International Challenge. London: University of London, Athlone Press.

CASPARI, I. (1976) Troublesome Children in Class. London: Routledge and Kegan Paul.

CLARKE, A.M. and CLARKE, A.D.B. (1979) Early experience: its limited effect upon later development. In Shaffer, R. and Dunn J. (eds). The First Years of Life. London: Wiley.

COMBER, L.C. and WHITFIELD, R.C. (1979) Action on Indiscipline: A Practical Guide for Teachers. Hemel Hampstead: National Association of Schoolmasters and the Association of Women Teachers.

CORRIGAN, P. (1979) Schooling the Smash Street Kids. London: Macmillan Press.

COULBY, D. and HARPER, T. (1981) ILEA D.O.5. Schools Support Unit. Evaluation: Phase 1. Unpublished.

CROWTHER, G. (1979) Units for disruptives: a behavioural approach to management. Contact, ILEA, 26 Jan. 1979.

CUMBRIA EDUCATION DEPARTMENT (1976) No Small Change. The Report of the Working Party on Problem Children in Schools.

DAVIE, R., BUTLER, N. and GOLDSTEIN, H. (1972) From Birth to Seven: A report of the National Child Development Study. London: Longmans.

DAVIES, J. (1981) Perspectives on Attendance. RS 749/80. Obtainable from H. Pennell, A 312, ILEA, The County Hall, London SE1 7PB.

DAWSON, R.L. (1980) Special Provision for Disturbed Pupils: a survey. London: Macmillan Education.

DEPARTMENT OF EDUCATION AND SCIENCE (1979) Aspects of Secondary Education in England: A survey by HM Inspectors of schools. H.M.S.O.

DEPARTMENT OF THE ENVIRONMENT (1978), National Dwelling and Housing Survey H.M.S.O.

DEVINE, P. (1980) Support Centres Programme Monitoring Study: First annual report. RS 744/80. Obtainable from H. Pennell, A312, ILEA, The County Hall, London, SE1 7PB.

DHSS (1976) Fit for the Future. Report of the Committee on Child Health Services. (The Court Report) H.M.S.O.

DIERENFIELD, R.B. (1982) Classroom Disruption in English Comprehensive Schools. Macalester College, St Paul, Minnesota.

FORD, J., MONGON, D. and WHELAN, M. (1982) Special Education and Social Control: Invisible Disasters. London: Routledge and Kegan Paul.

FOSTER, G. and Appleton, M. (1982) Special education in Holland. British Journal of Special Education. 9. No. 2

GALLOWAY, D. (1976) Case Histories in Classroom Management. London: Longmans.

GALLOWAY, D. (1979) Behavioural Units. A paper presented to the project's advisory committee. City of Sheffield Education Department.

GALLOWAY, D. and GOODWIN, C. (1979) Educating Slow-Learning and Maladjusted Children: Integration or Segregation. London: Longmans.

GALLOWAY, D., BAll, T., BLOMFIELD, D. and SEYD, R. (1982) *Schools and Disruptive Pupils.* London: Longman Group

GALTON, M., SIMON, B. and CROLL, P. (1980) *Inside the Primary School.* London: Routledge and Kegan Paul.

GILLHAM, B. (ed.) (1981) *Problem Behaviour in the Secondary School* London: Croom Helm.

GOLBY, M. (1979) Special units:some educational issues. *Journal of the Socialist Education Association,* 6, No. 2, Summer 1979.

GRUNSELL, R. (1978) *Born to be Invisible.* London: Macmillan Education.

GRUNSELL, R. (1980) *Beyond Control? Schools and Suspension.* London: Writers and Readers.

HARGREAVES, D. (1967) *Social Relations in a Secondary School.* London: Routledge and Kegan Paul.

HARGREAVES, D., HESTOR, S. and MELLOR, F. (1975) *Deviance in Classrooms.* London: Routledge and Kegan Paul.

HEGARTY, S., POCKLINGTON, K. and LUCAS, D. (1981) *Educating Pupils with Special Needs in the Ordinary School.* Windsor, Berks: NFER-Nelson.

H.M. Inspectorate of Schools (1978) *Behavioural Units: a survey of special units for pupils with behavioural problems.* London: Department of Education and Science.

H.M. Inspectorate of Schools (1978) *Truancy and Behaviour Problems in some Urban Schools.* London: Department of Education and Science.

H.M. Inspectorate of Schools (1979) *Aspects of Secondary Education in England.* London: H.M.S.O.

HOGHUGHI, M. (1978) *Troubled and Troublesome.* London: Burnett Books.

ILEA (1983) <u>Achievement in Schools.</u> Text of seminar given by P. Mortimore on 22 October 1981. ILEA.

JENNINGS, A. (ed) (1979) <u>Discipline in Primary and Secondary Schools Today.</u> London: Ward Lock Educational.

JONES-DAVIES, C. and CAVE, R. (eds) (1976) <u>The Disruptive Pupil in the Secondary School.</u> London: Ward Lock Educational.

KOUNIN, J.S. (1970) <u>Discipline and Group Management in Classrooms.</u> New York: Holt, Rinehart and Winston.

KYRIACOU, C. and SUTCLIFFE, J. (1978) Teacher stress: prevalence, sources and symptoms. <u>British Journal of Educational Psychology,</u> <u>48,</u> 159-167.

KYSEL, F. and VARLAAM, A. (1983) <u>The Child at School: A new behaviour schedule.</u> Unpublished.

LACEY, C. (1970) <u>Hightown Grammar.</u> Manchester: University of Manchester Press.

LASLETT, R. (1977) <u>Educating Maladjusted Children.</u> London: Granada.

LAWRENCE, J. (1981) <u>Exploring Techniques for coping with Disruptive Behaviour in Schools.</u> University of London, Goldsmiths' College, Educational Studies Monographs.

LAWRENCE, J., STEED, D. and YOUNG, P. (1978) Non-observational monitoring of disruptive behaviour in school. <u>Research Intelligence,</u> <u>4,</u> No. 1, 38.

LAWRENCE, J., STEED, D. and YOUNG, P. (1980) Local Authorities and autonomous off-site units for disruptive pupils in Secondary Schools. <u>Cambridge Journal of Education,</u> <u>10,</u> No. 2, 55-70.

LITTLE, A. (1977) What is happening in inner city schools? In FIELD, F. (ed.) <u>Education and</u>

the Urban Crisis. London: Routledge and Kegan Paul, pp. 64-89.

LLOYD-SMITH, M. (1979) The meaning of special units. Socialism and Education, 6.

LOWENSTEIN, L.F. (1972) Violence in Schools and its Treatment. Hemel Hempstead, Herts: National Association of Schoolmasters.

MARSHALL, T., FAIRHEAD, S., MURPHY, D. and ILES, S. (1978) Evaluation for Democracy. Home Office Research Unit. Unpublished.

MORTIMORE, J. and BLACKSTONE, T. (1982) Disadvantage and Education. London: Heinemann Educational.

MORTIMORE, J. and MORTIMORE, P. (1983) '"Helpful Servants" or "Dominating Master": a Critique of the Secondary Schools Examination System.' London: Institute of Education, University of London. Bedford Way Paper. In press.

NEWELL, P. (1980) Sin bins: the integration argument. Where, 160, August 1980.

NEWSAM, P. (1979) The school system's response to bad behaviour. Howard Journal, 18, 108-113.

O'HARE, E. (1980) Lancashire Disruptive Pupil Units. University of Lancaster: Centre for Educational Research and Development.

PARRY, K. (1976) Disruptive children in school: the view of a class teacher and head of house. In Jones-Davies, C. and Cave, R. (eds). The Disruptive Pupil in the Secondary School. London: Ward Lock Educational.

PAYNE, J. (1980) Disruptive Units in a Local Authority. M.A. Thesis, University of London.

RAVEN, J. (1979) An abuse of psychology for political purposes. Bulletin of the British Psychological Society, 32, 173-177.

REYNOLDS, D. (1975) When teachers and pupils refuse a truce - the secondary school and the generation of delinquency. In Mungham, G. and Pearson, G. (eds). British Working Class Youth Culture. London: Routledge and Kegan Paul.

ROBINSON, P. (1981) Perspectives on the Sociology of Education: An introduction. London: Routledge and Kegan Paul.

RUTTER, M. (1975) Helping Troubled Children. Harmondsworth, Middlesex: Penguin Books.

RUTTER, M. (1979) Changing Youth in a Changing Society: Patterns of adolescent development and disorder. The Rock Carling Fellowship, Nuffield Provincial Hospitals Trust.

RUTTER, M. and GRAHAM, P. (1966) Psychiatric Disorder in 10- and 11-year-old Children. Proceedings of the Royal Society of Medicine, 59, 382-7.

RUTTER, M., TIZARD, J. and WHITMORE, K. (1970) Education, Health and Behaviour. London: Longman Group.

RUTTER, M., COX, A., TUPLING, C., BERGER, M. and YULE, W. (1975) Attainment and adjustment in two geographical areas: I - The prevalence of psychiatric disorder. British Journal of Psychiatry, 126, 493-509.

RUTTER, M., MAUGHAN, B., MORTIMORE, P. and OUSTON, J. (1979) Fifteen Thousand Hours: secondary schools and their effects on children. London: Open Books.

SHIPMAN, M. (1980) The limits of positive discrimination. In Marland, M. (ed) Education for the Inner City. London: Heinemann.

SMITH, D. (1979) Slow Learners and the Secondary School Curriculum. In D. RUBINSTEIN (ed) Education and Equality. Harmondsworth: Penguin Books.

Bibliography

STEED, D.M., LAWRENCE, J. and YOUNG, P. (1982) Monitoring of disruptive behaviour and implications for Inset. British Journal of In-Service Education, 89-93, Spring 1982.

STERNE, M. (1981) The answer to disruptives? Education p.9, 28 Aug. 1981.

ST-JOHN BROOKS, C. (1981) What should schools do with their problem children? New Society, p44, 8 Jan. 1981.

TATTUM, D. (1982) Disruptive Pupils in Schools and Units. New York: John Wiley and Sons.

TAWNEY, D. (ed) (1976) Curriculum Evaluation Today: Trends and Implications Schools Council Research Studies. London: Macmillan Education.

THORNBURY, R. (1978) The Changing Urban School. London: Methuen.

TOPPING, K.J. (1983) Educational systems for disruptive adolescents. Beckenham, Kent : Croom Helm.

UPTON, G. and GOBELL, A. (1980) Behaviour Problems in the Comprehensive School. Cardiff University: Faculty of Education.

VARLAAM, A. (1974) Educational attainment and behaviour at school. In Russell, C. et al. (eds). Greater London Intelligence Quarterly, 29, December 1974. London: Greater London Council.

WHITE, R. (1980) Absent with Cause. London: Routledge and Kegan Paul.

WIGLEY, V. (1980) Personal communication.

WILLIAMS, P. (ed) (1974) Behaviour Problems in School. London: Hodder and Stoughton.

WILLIS, P. (1977) Learning to Labour. Farnborough: Saxon House.

WILSON, M. and EVANS, M. (1980) Education of Disturbed Pupils. London: Methuen Educational.

WOODS, J. (1981) Disruptive Pupils: a discussion of the issues raised in the literature concerning the education and treatment of disruptive pupils. Unpublished.

YOUNG, P., LAWRENCE, J. and STEED, D. (1979) Local Education Authority responses to disruptive behaviour: a research note. Policy and Politics, 7, 387-393.

YOUNG, P., STEED, D. and LAWRENCE, J. (1980) Local Education Authorities and autonomous off-site units for disruptive pupils in secondary schools. Cambridge Journal of Education, 10, No. 2.

YULE, W. (1969) Maladjustment and reading difficulties: the findings of the Isle of Wight studies. Remedial Education, 4, No. 3, 124-128.

INDEX